The Dragon'

A play

Douglas Watkinson

Samuel French – London
New York – Sydney – Toronto – Hollywood

THE DRAGON'S TAIL

First presented in London by Pencon Productions Ltd and Toby Rowland for Libby Productions Ltd by arrangement with Louis Benjamin for Stoll Moss Theatres Ltd, at the Apollo Theatre on 21st October, 1985, with the following cast of characters:

Mary	Penelope Keith
Frank	Mark Kingston
Dylan	Robert Hines
Apricot	Amanda Root

The play directed by Michael Rudman
Designed by Carl Toms with Bruce Snyder

The action takes place in a clearing by a wooded lakeside in North Wales in late summer

ACT I Scene 1 Midnight, Friday
        Scene 2 9 a.m., Saturday

ACT II Scene 1 Twenty minutes later
         Scene 2 Half an hour later

Time—the present

PRODUCTION NOTE

By using a light van, such as a Honda or Suzuki, without an engine, it should be fairly easy to manipulate on stage. However, please refer to page 51 where a note concerning re-staging some of the van's entrances and exits can be found.

ACT I*

SCENE 1

A clearing by a wooded lakeside in North Wales. Late summer. Midnight

The stage is set in a semi-circle of Celtic foliage with access to a treacherous winding track off L. Far upstage is a bank over which, we presume, is the lake itself. Even farther beyond is a backdrop depicting the Cambrian mountains. Slightly R of C is a low, lightweight tent, just large enough to sleep two people. It is zipped up and pegged down against the storm

When the CURTAIN rises a storm is raging, with occasional lightning giving us a ghostly view of this soggy beauty spot. For several moments we listen to the storm but it soon gives way to the approach of a van of some sort. Indeed, headlights can be seen sweeping across the clearing as dangerous corners are taken with much crashing of gears. Eventually the vehicle gets to within several yards of the clearing and the engine stalls and dies

A few moments pass. The engine is fired several times but to no avail

A voice calls out above the storm

Mary (*off*) Frank . . . we've stopped.
Frank (*off, angrily*) I know! Petrol!

A van door opens, then slams shut

(*off*) Sou'wester! Cape!
Mary (*off*) Please.
Frank (*off*) Please!
Mary (*off*) There's no point in getting in a tizz. What did I say in Harlech? I said petrol. Any second now you'll blame me for . . .
Frank (*off*) Am I blaming you? Are you deaf? Are you hearing things?
Mary (*off*) Clever as I am, I cannot hear things if I'm deaf. Hadn't we better pull off the road? And drill for oil?

Frank enters L backwards, measuring with eyes and hands the amount of space available for his van to reverse into. He is a man in his mid-forties, dressed in a yellow cycling cape and a sou'wester

---

* N.B. Paragraph 3 on page ii of this Acting Edition regarding photocopying and video-recording should be carefully read.

A sudden flash of lightning illuminates the stage and Frank's fear

   With a yell that can only be spelled "Aaaargh" Frank exits L in haste

A van door opens then slams shut again. Frank has got back into the van

Mary (*off*) What the hell are you *doing*?
Frank (*off*) I'll steer. You push. (*Angrily*) Not me, you daft bitch, the *van*!
Mary (*off, sighing wearily*) It was a little joke, Frank. Where are my
   waterproofs? God knows why the Amazons only cut off *one* breast. Their
   menfolk obviously lost the secateurs or whatever they used. How do I
   look?
Frank (*off*) Jesus Christ, girl, there's only sheep out there! Right, out and
   push!
Mary (*off*) Anywhere special? Camden Town?

The van door opens and slams shut again

Frank (*off*) Back into that clearing. Come on, girl, get your shoulder to it!

   *Gradually a light van enters, backwards, from L. Frank is at the steering
   wheel giving suitable encouragement*

   Come on! Come on! Bloody great girl your size should have no problem!
   That's the girl! Heave! (*. . . And other polite encouragements*)

   *Mary enters, pushing the van from the front, her body at an angle to the
   ground, her shoulder to the radiator. The van is a clapped-out, knocked-up
   makeshift caravan . . . the work of a man who is basically cautious, if not
   slightly mean. And for our purposes it doesn't even need an engine*

*As the back of the van reaches the tent a flash or two of lightning illuminates
the horror to come. The van rips into the tent and flattens it completely and
comes to rest directly over the remains*

Frank (*yelling*) That'll do. (*He slams on the brakes*)

Mary flattens against the nose of the van

Mary (*drily*) Super brakes.

Frank jumps out and comes round to Mary

Frank Well done, girl! Everything OK?
Mary Apart from nearly joining you in the front as a bag of chips.

Frank smiles and pecks her on the cheek

Frank What time is it? (*He moves to dowse the headlights*)

Mary checks her watch in the headlights just as Frank dowses them

Mary Quarter to twelve.

*The rain has stopped and Mary removes her sou'wester revealing a face that is
full of a girlish sense of humour. At this particular stage in her life Mary has
two problems which aren't necessarily related. Firstly she drinks far too much*

and secondly her mouth outstrips her brain with an overbearing, witty fluency. But not too deeply buried beneath her grand, verbal gymnastics is a warm, though childless, woman

Frank is the perfect foil for her. He is willing to be both parent and child and survives her frequent onslaughts with dry wit and much good sense. The latter is not yet apparent . . .

Shall we ring for the AA? (*She pauses and qualifies, being a somewhat cut glass lady*) Or, on second thoughts, the RAC.

Frank It was the first thing I noticed about the place. The phone boxes.

There is a flash of lightning. Frank grabs Mary as he would his mother. He yells again what can only be spelled "Aaaargh!"

(*Almost immediately*) I'm sorry.

A clap of thunder makes Frank wince

Mary Silly boy! It's only Jesus moving his furniture.

Frank Does he have to do it in the rain? (*He slides open the side doors of the van and takes out a Calor gas lamp and lights it*)

Mary In my Father's house are many mansions. One of them's bound to have dodgy plumbing. If you just stop and think you'll find it all terribly romantic.

Frank Make yourself useful. Find out where we are.

Mary takes a map from the passenger seat and wanders a little way from the van. She makes an expansive gesture to the surrounding countryside, as if she would embrace it

Mary We're in Wales! Land of my fathers and their woad.

Frank Don't wander off! (*Drily*) There may be Druids in the phone boxes.

Mary Phoning their mothers. How sweet. (*She scrutinizes the map. It's an Ordnance Survey of the National Park, carefully folded and protected by a polythene bag*)

Frank removes his cape

Now let me see. . . . (*She can't. She looks up*) Hallo? Any chance of turning the moon up just a snatch?

The moon comes out from behind a cloud

(*Unimpressed but grateful*) Lovely job! Now, we turned off here. I said turn left so you immediately turned right. And carried on down this unmetalled, unadopted, unnumbered road, which you will be fascinated to know is also a bridle way. It seems to disappear into a lake. Llyn Cwm Bychan. What pretty names they have round here.

Frank Mary, please! We could be lost forever! And who will care! My daughter. My poor little girl. . . . (*He gets an enormous flask and pours them each a plastic flask top of tea*)

Mary She's twenty-five, built like a rhino and you loathe her. At our age, we should enjoy the moment.

Frank Which moment?

Mary (*with a grand gesture*) *This* one! The here and now!

Frank (*counting off one moment with his hand*) I enjoyed it. Now what do I do?

Mary Here we are, miles from anywhere, alone, together. We could have gone to Broadstairs and had people swarming all over us. We could be on a hot sweaty beach with people getting under our feet . . .

Frank trips on something

There you are, you see, you've stumbled across something of interest already. What is it?

Frank bends down and picks it up

Frank It's a tent peg.

Mary Now when did you last see one of those in Aylesbury?

Frank Do you think I should inform the Coroner? It could be treasure trove.

Mary Let's drink our tea and get to bed. Tomorrow is, as even you could work out, another day. We'll stop a passing peasant, beg some petrol off him and down the yellow brick road we'll go.

Frank trips on something else

Oh, for God's sake, Frank, do try to stay upright . . . !

Frank bends down and picks up another tent peg. He examines it, rather puzzled

Frank Another tent peg.

Mary So now you've got a matching pair.

Frank Mary . . . one peg is a coincidence. Two is a . . .

Mary . . . a mathematical wonder! There *is* a Roman camp marked on the map, but I thought they slept under their horses.

Frank looks under the van and sees the tent. He straightens up. In his own time he'll continue the scene with a quiet dignity

Frank Mary, you know that feeling of wishing you could turn the clock back?

Mary And correct the mistakes of one's youth? Oh yes.

Frank Or even the mistakes of, say, five minutes ago?

Mary I do.

Frank Good. To that end, there's something under the van.

Mary Yes, dear. Wales.

Frank Above Wales. Below the van.

There is a slight pause

Mary It's called a gap, Frank.

Frank (*pointing*) Tent.

Mary Pardon?

Frank We have ... *you* have ... pushed me and my van, which I was sitting in, which makes me only a *party* to any crime, over a tent!

Mary No, dear, one pushes people over an *edge*, not a tent.

Frank There! Look! What is it?

She bends at the waist and looks. She straightens up and smiles at Frank

Mary It's a *bungalow* tent! (*She galvanizes herself into action*) Drink up! Let's go! You steer! I'll push!

Frank But suppose they're ... and we've ...

Mary Frank, you are a doctor! Surely you've seen dead people before! (*She comes down to earth*) Oh my God! Get in the van!

Frank tries to scuttle in through the side doors. Mary hauls him back

Mary The *driver's* seat!

Frank Which way are we facing?

Mary points to the L exit. Frank goes round and gets in the driving seat. Mary goes to the back of the van and pushes it off the tent. Frank brings it to rest, L. He gets out and comes over to Mary. They both stand looking down at the wreckage. The lamp in Frank's hand judders with his fear. A slight pause

Mary I think this is something we should do together, don't you?

Frank No. I think you should do it on your own. I'll hold the lamp. We can't have killed anyone, can we? (*In the same breath*) What are the ... well ... lumps?

Mary They're either two rucksacks ...

Frank Good.

Mary ... or two people!

Frank No, don't. ...

Mary Maybe they did what hedgehogs do when they heard us coming.

Frank Farted?

Mary Curled themselves up into little balls prior to rolling away. (*With a false tremor in her voice*) And they never made it. (*She gets down on her knees and lifts the canvas to see the damage*) They are rucksacks.

Frank Yes, of course they are. ... Are you sure?

Mary And very expensive ones, if I know my rucksacks. ... Hold the lamp still, Frank.

Frank For me, this is still. ... (*He relaxes a little*) Do you know, if one thinks about it ... which I'm doing ... it is a bit of a cheek. People chucking tents up all over the place.

Mary (*still sorting through the stuff*) Ah! Smokers. (*She finds a cigarette packet and takes one from it*)

Frank No! (*He snatches it from her and throws it aside*)

Mary (*her eyes following the cigarette*) You filthy, stinking obnoxious weed. I loathe and detest you.

Frank Me or the fag?

Mary My mother told me the only way to give up cigarettes was to be rude to them.

Frank That was twenty years ago.

Mary One must persevere. Oh dear, the pole. (*She shows it to him in two halves. ... She takes the top half, lifts the apex of the tent and, jokingly, places it in position*) Do you think they'd notice?

Frank We could have killed them you know. Who do they think they are burdening us with that? Who are they, Mary? Who?

Mary How the hell do I know who we haven't killed! They're probably a young couple, carefree, irresponsible ... all their lives in front of them.

Frank How dare they! *You* were perfectly justified in getting *me* to pull off the road and *forcing* me to back into this clearing.

To her delight, Mary finds a bottle of vodka

Mary Ah, a kindred spirit ...

Frank takes the bottle from her, laying it aside

Frank We could've killed them.

Mary Do you know, I believe you're sorry we didn't. Next year we'll go to Gilwell Park and drive all over the scouts. Ah! One of them is male, the other is female. I really should take this up for a living. (*She holds up a skirt she has plucked from the debris*) Expensive and vulgar. (*She sniffs the surrounding air like a basset hound*) Like the aftershave.

Frank That girl wears aftershave? (*He apologizes for the absurd observation almost immediately*) Sorry.

Mary Kids, Frank. One of each gender.

Frank Late back! By God, if they were mine they'd know about it!

Mary If they'd been early, they would now be the biggest pizza fillings in the world.

Frank I'm one of those people who *does* believe everything he hears about youth. They're immoral, violent, and usually bigger than me. And that's my fault. All those years prescribing vitamins and counselling dried eggs.

Mary I'm immoral, violent and bigger than you.

Frank Yes, and look where you've landed me! Trapped in a foreign country where every time they speak they water your lawn. With a woman who refuses to push my car to ... Camden Town ...

Mary stands up and they kiss as old friends do

Mary We shall hit the plywood, badly made bunks, Frank ... grab what zeds we can and, in the morning, make peace with these immoral, violent, giants. I will do the talking and you will nod your head thus ... (*she nods*) ... and be impressed. Now go and change and I'll promise not to laugh.

Frank You're enjoying this, aren't you?

Mary For the first time in your life, you're absolutely right.

Frank Poor old Mary. If I had a textbook with me I'd look you up. You're bound to be curable. Everything is these days.

Frank goes behind the van to change. Mary reaches in through the sliding doors and finds her own holdall and a bright orange picnic box. She opens the latter and takes out a sandwich

Sooner or later we'll be out of business, doctors. Plug your symptoms into a home computer and off to the chemist with the print-out. (*A secondary thought*) I hope all this doesn't frighten you, by the way.

Mary (*to herself*) Or else who's to look after poor Frank? (*She holds up a sandwich*) You filthy, stinking, obnoxious calories, I loathe and detest you. (*She bites into it immediately, then sneaks over to the remains of the tent and finds the bottle of vodka. She returns to the van quickly*)

Frank What are you doing? Mary, you've not drifted off, have you?

Mary Only in a manner of speaking. (*She takes the top off the bottle, pours a measure into the cap and knocks it back like someone who's done the same thing all too often. It being night time she has probably been boozing all day and is well and truly topped up*) Frank.

Frank Yes?

Mary You'll never know how *glad* I am that I've stopped drinking.

Frank Didn't I tell you? I mean if your liver was off Land's End they'd stick a lighthouse on it.

Mary He loves me, he loves me not, he loves me. . . . (*She takes another shot of the vodka and closes her eyes as she swills it around in her mouth*)

Frank Talk to me, Mary.

Mary I'm cleaning my teeth. (*She gargles and swallows*)

Frank I've been thinking too, you know. With any luck they won't even notice us when they come back. I mean we didn't notice *them*.

Mary (*to herself*) Immoral, violent, large *and* thick. (*She considers returning the vodka bottle to the remains of the tent but decides against it. She places it furtively in her holdall*)

Frank emerges from behind the van in his pyjamas and a very old tartan dressing-gown. He wears leather slippers

Mary (*looking at him with restraint*) Has the dressing-gown been in the family long?

Frank I'm not so sure it's a good idea, me getting all kitted out for bed you know. Suppose they come in the middle of the night.

Mary They wouldn't hit a man dressed like that.

Frank I admire your faith, Mary. I really do. But you don't know kids . . . they're not all they're cracked up to be. But how could you possibly understand?

Mary (*furiously*) I'm getting rather *tired* of this myth about the childless!

Frank (*wearily*) Now don't start all that again. You'll only upset yourself.

Mary If you haven't had thirty children by the time you're four the only people you can talk to are vicars, eunuchs and houseplants!

Frank And the odd doctor. (*He gets into the van and disappears from view*)

Mary Oh yes . . . the odd doctor indeed. I've had your opinion about children rammed down my throat for the past twenty years. It's been so persistent, so monotonous, it's almost a part of me.

Frank Taught you something, then. You should be grateful. . . .

Mary (*leaning into the van and yelling*) So is it your opinion or my sterility that's half killed me, I wonder? (*She leaves Frank alone, preferring her own company. She imitates him for a few sentences*) "Children, Mary, you wouldn't believe how childish they are. They rearrange your furniture and open your mail; they come in for a chat about nuclear war when you're having a bath; they expect to be picked up in the middle of the night and ferried from one party to another, hundreds of miles away. They trail dirty laundry through the house. Silk shirts end up polishing ten year old cars. They speak like the wolf children, in a language you don't understand. They dye their hair grey as soon as they can. Overnight, beautiful blond tresses are replaced by Lancashire grey. They pluck their eyelashes, they're rude to your parents, they pick their toe nails with their socks on. They blackmail you for straight cash and never pay you back. If you dare to mention it they punish you by stealing from your wallet. They fail to give you important phone messages. Sometimes they smell, yet even so they have ... well ... goings on with people you've never met. They drink. They smoke. They're ashamed of you ... why else would they ask you to wait outside pubs when you go to collect them, having just finished their homework for them? In a crowd they always lose you, but by God when you pass a record shop, there they are, right by your side. Smiling. They eat strange things. Their fads change from day to day ... vegetarian, carnivore, vegan, fish and chips, starvation, all in the space of a week. Yet they know all the best restaurants in town. They can read a wine list but never a book. They order things they've never had at home. And nor have you. Venison, smoked salmon, pheasant. They never, never say thank you. Then they leave home and you never see them again because you've moaned and groaned at every twist and turn of their youth. And somehow you didn't mean to." (*Pause*) Says Frank. But Mary says, "Don't they sound fun!"

Dylan and Apricot, holding hands, enter R. *Dylan is, by nature, a peacemaker to Apricot's human hand grenade, but that is not to say he is without fire or that she doesn't possess a gentle, feminine side. Right now, for reasons to become clear at the end of the scene, Apricot is as high as a kite and Dylan is desperate to keep hold of the string*

Mary notices them, but as if they were part of her monologue. She looks up and smiles at them ...

Dylan (*smiling back at her*) And Mary is right.
Mary Yes, dear. She invariably is. (*She comes to and realizes who they must be*) Frank. Frank!
Dylan No, Dylan ...
Mary Bob or Thomas?
Dylan No ... just Dylan. This is Apricot.
Apricot Hi!
Mary That must be youthspeak for "Good-evening, how are you?"

Frank emerges from the van

Ah Frank, the tall one is Dylan, the midget is Apricot. (*To Dylan*) Your mother certainly had big plans for *you* didn't she? (*To Apricot*) But how did yours see her daughter? As fruit, Frank, fruit. But have no fear, dear, we shall emerge from the twentieth century as the eaters, not the eaten.

Apricot moves to the remains of the tent and looks down at it

Apricot Jesus Christ! Look at this, Dill! We could've been asleep in there!
Mary Oh yes, but I think you'd have woken up by now, don't you?
Apricot (*holding up the remains of a leather jacket*) Staying long?
Mary Oh, back and forth, you know.
Apricot Long enough to write out a cheque for two hundred and eighty quid?
Mary Two hundred and eighty? For a piece of chamois leather? Darling, you've been robbed.
Apricot (*to Frank*) I take it this old bat's with you.
Frank (*laughing*) Yes. We're inseparable.
Mary Bat? Moi?
Apricot (*to Frank*) So are you *both* crazy or just her?
Mary Frank, I've known this young lady for thirty seconds and already I dislike her. Is that medically possible?
Frank (*to Dylan; of Mary*) She's a heavy drinker. From Aylesbury.
Apricot Oh, enough *said*. I'm sorry for making you so rude to me.
Mary And yet she has a certain grace. A trifle short perhaps, but . . .

Dylan and Apricot both look down at the tent

Apricot (*salty*) But?
Mary But isn't this a beautiful part of the world?
Dylan Isn't it just. Do you know, I could've sworn there was an elevation here when we left.
Mary There was, dear. The changing face of Britain . . . living sculpture. A new land mass here . . . a fresh depression there. (*She points at the tent*)
Dylan It was a polite way of asking, "What have you done to my tent?"
Mary You see, Frank, he's not a thug at all. He's most gentlemanly. We knocked it down.
Frank (*pointing at Mary*) *She* did. I was in the van. She was pushing.
Mary But we wouldn't have done if it hadn't been in the way.
Apricot There are two thousand square miles of National Park to play in. Why pick on us?
Mary (*drawing herself up*) Now don't get uppity with me, Nectarine, It was a simple mistake.
Apricot Could've happened to anyone?
Mary Was that sympathy or sarcasm? The latter in a young girl is most unbecoming, don't you agree?
Apricot This was our home!
Mary You live here? They're didecoys, Frank. Plundering the Welfare State, making a *fortune* in white heather and clothes pegs . . .
Frank I think a good night's sleep'd do us all . . .
Apricot No, we don't bloody well live here!
Mary (*sharply*) Then why get our relationship off to a bad start by lying and swearing, Greengage?

Apricot Stop that!

Dylan (*reasonably*) Now listen, folks ... why don't we all stop ...

Mary Don't you strike that matey pose with me, young man.

Apricot They're nutters, Dill.

Frank (*laughing, matily*) No, no ... I'm a doctor. (*And adds, as if it explains everything*) From Aylesbury. Where the ducks come from.

Apricot Fair enough, duck. Ever performed major surgery on a tent? Now's your chance to break new ground. ... Where's my vodka?

Mary (*as at a funeral*) It was the only casualty, I assure you. It evaporated.

Apricot Out through the pores in your skin, I'll bet.

Mary She has a wit, Frank. I don't like it, but she does have one.

Dylan (*among the remains*) My razor!

Frank He's going to kill us! I knew it!

Dylan Not with a twelve volt battery, Frank.

Frank (*feeling daft*) Sorry ...

Apricot (*to Frank*) How the hell did you *manage* it?

Frank Well it all started way back in Aylesbury. (*And from now on most references to Aylesbury are muted*) ... She wanted to retire. A cottage in the country. So she stuck her finger in the *AA Book of the Road* and said "Wales".

Dylan Retire? How old is she?

Mary You see, now Dylan's got it right. He wants to get to know me properly. I'm forty-two dear. How old are you?

Dylan Twenty-one next birthday.

Mary (*smiling*) That makes me worth exactly two of you. What a wonderful age. The key to the bivouac and all that.

Apricot Dill, let's get in the car and scoot. We'll sort this out in the morning. Dill!

Mary Blackberry darling, you shouldn't shorten his name. You make him sound as if he belongs in a herb garden.

Apricot He shortens me!

Mary To Apric ... ? (*Pause. She apologizes for the vulgarity*) I'm so sorry.

Apricot (*coldly*) To Ape.

There is a slight pause

Mary Yes ... well that's understandable.

Apricot I've heard all the jokes about my name! A thousand times! You mow us down with your clapped out load of old iron! You blame us for being in the way! And from then on take the piss out of us! Did you never hear of the word "sorry"?

And, being a doctor, Frank recognizes true hysteria when it rears its head, as now with Apricot

Frank (*of Mary*) Would it make any difference if I apologized on her behalf?

Apricot Yes it would. It'd make you look a fool. Why can't she do it for herself?

There is a slight pause

Frank I suppose that's a very good question.

Mary *If* she were calm, controlled and gracious I would have no hesitation.

Apricot breaks away from Dylan, grabs Mary by the lapels and tries to shake her

Apricot Do you know what we've been through lately? Do you?

Mary Look at this, Frank. Physical contact already. (*To Apricot*) How can I *possibly* know? And take your hands off me or I shall wop you into yonder thicket.

Apricot Yeah? Yeah?

Mary The word does have an "S" on the end of it, giving us "Yes". (*She clouts Apricot round the side of the head*)

Apricot recoils a few yards, but remains on her feet

Well . . . perhaps not the thicket. But next time.

Apricot She hit me!

Mary Why the note of surprise in your voice? Frank, please examine the fruit for damage and if you find none I think we should all retire to bed. We can fight much better in the morning when we can see each other.

Frank Right.

Apricot Don't you come near me! Keep him away Dill!

Dylan Now I think we should all calm down. Or is that a silly suggestion?

Mary Dylan, Frank is fully insured and I am a superb liar of many years' standing. Commercial Union will *weep* to learn that our Japanese car . . . the Japanese bit is good psychology . . . which of us really believes that Hirohito is dead? Our Japanese car, how dare it, committed your British trailer tent, your Harrods li-los and gold lamé sleeping-bags to a grave beneath the Celtic sod. More tragic still, a crate of vintage malt whisky . . . (*she pauses to lick her lips*) . . . shattered and seeped into the ground. As evidence we shall produce photos of that tree staggering about being breathalysed. Is it a deal?

Dylan (*doubtfully*) Well . . .

Mary Good. (*She takes his hand and shakes it, then says one of her many lines in parenthesis*) Oh dear, you bite your nails. (*She drops his hand and returns to the main tack*) As for tonight's sleeping arrangements, we shall tuck up together in the van. Does that meet with your approval, Dylan?

Dylan Well, it's a bit of a . . .

Mary Then perhaps you'd ask Apricot to abandon the street urchin in her for the sake of a good night's sleep.

Apricot (*moody but severely*) The answer's no.

Mary turns to her, preparatory to putting her down as far as she will go

Mary Apricot, please don't think me unsympathetic. I see in you the folly of my own childhood. Unprovoked tantrums, appalling dress sense and make-up applied by a Sioux Indian in distress.

Dylan (*defending Apricot*) Now hang on a tick . . .

Mary Dylan, you are *bound* to defend her, I know, but face the truth now and spare yourself pain later on. In loco parentis I have just given Apricot a thick ear. If her mother had done so ten years ago we should all be friends by now. Weakness in a mother is the root cause of every problem in the Western World. Yet ... and this proves how understanding a creature I can be ... if the mother is an absolute slut, what chance does the daughter stand?

There is a slight pause

Apricot screams in anger, turns and exits L

Dylan (*calling after her as a reflex*) Ape!

Mary is bewildered by Apricot's behaviour but remains steadfast

Mary (*eventually*) Well ... I think that proves my point. Frank, run after her and give her a tablet.

Frank (*dismayed by Mary's attack on Apricot*) Don't you think it'll look a bit strange? A highly respected GP chasing a young girl through Wales in his pyjamas?

Mary affects a weariness with Frank's stupidity

Mary (*sighing*) Frank, sheep have always made very bad witnesses. (*Sharply*) Just go!

Dylan catches him by the arm and holds him fast

Dylan (*quietly furious*) Hold it! Let's keep this nice and verbal, shall we?
Mary I tried to. Indeed I'm still willing ...
Dylan (*impatiently*) Fine! I've dealt with cut glass bullies before Mary ...
Mary (*put out*) I think you'd better call me Mrs Challis.
Dylan ... and the one and only thing they respond to is fear. (*Dragging Frank with him, he advances on Mary who remains unperturbed*)
Frank (*quickly, quietly*) She *doesn't* but I *do*!
Dylan You have the style, grace and brains of a performing dinosaur! My lawyer will sort out the details and no ... we will not lie to any insurance company!
Mary You're overwrought. In the morning you'll see things in a much more crooked light. Meanwhile ... Apricot ...
Dylan (*shouting for the first time*) Apricot will be fine! Shorter than you she may be but what you lack in brains she makes up for in spine.
Frank (*still in Dylan's grip*) Hadn't I better check her all the same?
Dylan You'll find her in a lay-by, fifty yards up the road, in our car which is also foreign, which we also backed off the road without even damaging a twig!
Mary Well there's no need to boast about it. But isn't it strange how our enemies' cars are very good at going backwards. Is this why we won the war, one asks? Do go and see to her, Frank. Take your bag and a torch. You and I will remain professional even if these two scruffs don't.
Frank (*smiling at Dylan*) I shall need both arms.

Dylan lets go of him

  Frank goes to the van, takes his doctor's bag and a torch and exits R *quickly*

Mary You see ... the doctor in him is really quite brave, even though the human being is a coward. (*Pause. Quietly*) You haven't got a cigarette on you by any chance?

Dylan takes a packet from his pocket and throws them down at Mary's feet. Conscious of being undignified, she stoops down, picks the packet up and takes out a cigarette

  (*Casually*) Match?

Dylan beckons with his forefinger and she approaches. He lights her cigarette then catches her by the arm before she can take a second puff

Dylan Still not afraid ... ?
Mary Yes I am. It's quite exciting. ... (*She smiles at him*)
Dylan (*in a quiet and sinister manner*) A thousand years ago, Mrs Challis, I would've killed you for upsetting Ape ...
Mary And made me yet another martyr to the truth? (*A beat. One almost believes her next line*) What *did* I say?
Dylan (*quietly*) Her mother ...
Mary Oh yes ... that. (*She gets the vodka from her holdall and pours a measure. She knocks it back*) You're right ... it's her mother I should be feeling sorry for. And you.
Dylan She lost her mother two months ago.
Mary (*replacing the bottle and making a grand gesture*) Come the dawn we shall rise up like a gang of phoenixes and look for her.

Dylan scoffs

  If we have to comb the National Park blade of grass by glade of brass we shall find her. ... I was very good at orienteering as a girl. Where was she last seen?
Dylan In the mortuary at Nottingham.

A pause. Mary's brain has caught up with her mouth. She turns away to mentally kick herself

Mary You mean lost as in ...
Dylan As in forever. ...
Mary Oh!

There is a pause. Mary turns back to Dylan

Dylan Lost for words, Mrs Challis? Well now ... history in the making.
Mary (*sharply*) Why ever didn't you say, you wretched boy!
Dylan Have you ever tried stopping you in full flood?
Mary (*nodding*) Yes ... well ... now you've got to help me.
Dylan (*amused and amazed*) I believe you mean it too!
Mary My mouth. I've always had trouble with it. (*And it was a joke which had no effect on Dylan*) How long have you been married?

Dylan I'm not.

Mary (*giggling, to signal another joke*) Oh, I see . . . you just *camp* together. (*Seriously*) Oh Dylan, please don't be severe. Can't you see what a mess I am . . . ?

Dylan (*taking the bottle from her*) Sure can Mrs Challis. (*He puts the bottle in the van*) The kind of mess you won't get out of too easily, without a spine like Apricot's.

Mary She's lucky to have you.

Dylan (*lightly, but very conscious of the effect he's about to have*) She's had me for seventeen years. I'm her brother. Goodnight, Mrs Challis. Sleep badly.

Dylan exits R

Mary (*calling*) Dylan! Please wait! (*But there's no response. She shrugs in annoyance at her own stupidity, goes to the bottle, takes another measure, then knocks it back. She speaks softly and angrily*) Stupid great bitch! (*She smiles wearily*) God, is that the worst you can say about yourself? (*Angry at the world again*) Ah, to hell with it! (*She pours herself another measure and crooks her elbow as if she's about to knock it back. To the vodka*) You filthy, stinking, obnoxious fluid, I hate you! (*She looks at it, debating whether to chuck it or drink it. To the vodka*) But not a lot. . . . (*She knocks it back*)

CURTAIN

SCENE 2

The same. It is early morning, bright and sunny if a little chilly

When the CURTAIN *rises Frank is on stage alone and has already cooked a breakfast of far too many bacon sandwiches. Tea has been brewed in an enormous pot. Two camping chairs are by the van. As he cuts the extremely thick sandwiches, Frank seems at ease with the world and is singing to himself*

Frank   Woad's the stuff to show men,
              Woad to scare your foe-men,
              Boil it blue, and strain it through,
              And rub it on your chest and your abdomen,
              Men of Harle . . .
              (*His voice tails off as . . .*)

Dylan enters, carrying a large black dustbin liner

Frank (*rising and holding out a hand to Dylan*) Dylan, your mother. I'm so sorry.

Dylan (*shaking the offered hand*) Thanks. (*He goes to the remains of the disaster and begins to put things into the bin liner, kneeling down to do so*)

Frank (*returning to the bread*) Doesn't matter how old you are. Nineteen or ninety. When your mother goes you really are on your own. (*He changes the mood of his speech upwards as he relaxes*) Anyway ... question now burdening me is should I have made bacon sandwiches for two or four?
Dylan So you compromised and catered for an army.
Frank Try me. (*He offers Dylan the plate*)

Dylan takes a sandwich, which must be an inch and a half thick at its lowest point, and examines it carefully

Dylan So that's why they call it Haute Cuisine.
Frank How's your sister?
Dylan Spark out. That pill you gave her did the trick. (*He smiles*) Sell us a bottle?
Frank Dylan, is your father still with us?
Dylan Possibly.
Frank Oh ... like that is it?
Dylan Where's Mary, Mary, downright bloody contrary?
Frank Avoiding making breakfast. You will wait and speak to her, won't you?
Dylan Well ... the plan *was* never to see her again ...
Frank ... only she has things to say. She was up most of the night, prowling around, blaming me of course. "How can I call myself a doctor if I can't even diagnose orphanitis?" (*Pause*) She was also very keen to know how you can afford a brand new Mercedes. So am I, come to that.
Dylan (*flatly*) I'm rich.

Frank waits for more explanation. It doesn't come

Frank Yes. Well that's a pretty full answer. Do you think I could syphon some petrol from it.
Dylan No good, I'm afraid. Diesel engine.
Frank Ah! Well that won't please her for a start. My fault again, of course. "Why couldn't we run over somebody rich with a *petrol* Mercedes?"

There is a slight pause

Dylan (*looking at Frank seriously*) You do know you needn't put up with all that, don't you?
Frank Sorry?
Dylan I almost believe you *don't*. (*Beat*) Frank ... I only caught a glimpse of it last night but ... well ... every time she opens her mouth you duck.
Frank (*unperturbed*) Yes. Fascinating you know. Wondering how she'll distort things next.
Dylan I'm being serious, Frank. You wouldn't be the first man to leave his wife stranded. (*He nods at the road*) Run away now, mate, divorce her at your leisure.
Frank (*with amusement*) Oh ... God, we're not married! Dear me, no. I'm not completely daft, you know ...
Dylan You mean you hang around her from *choice*? You should see a doctor.

Frank Don't trust 'em. (*He falls serious*) And you two are off? Where to?
Dylan Hadn't thought. Home probably.

There is a slight pause

Frank How long have you been driving round the country pretending that
your mother is only *slightly* dead?

Dylan is impressed that Frank has gone straight to the heart of the matter

Dylan Now you *are* clever. One hell of a bad cook, but clever . . .
Frank (*pouring Dylan a mug of tea*) Dylan . . . (*he smiles at him*) . . . do take
another bite so that you can't answer me back.

Dylan warms to Frank's humanity and bites into the doorstep

Do something for me. Just let her apologize to you and Apricot. You
don't have to accept it, just stand there while she says it. Be quite a new
experience for her, saying sorry.
Dylan *You* found her, Frank. *You* sort her out.
Frank Not as easy as it sounds. She's got no vocabulary for love or
sympathy . . . no words of softness . . . not yet. I live in hope that she'll
change of course . . .
Dylan She won't. And nor will you. The day she dies you'll still be
apologizing for her.
Frank (*knowing himself very well*) Habit? Love? What's the difference?
Dylan You don't love her . . . you're just scared to push her aside!
Frank (*smiling equably*) All that wisdom on one bacon sandwich. With a
nice piece of rump steak you could probably save the world.

Dylan returns to filling the bin liner

*Mary enters, L. She carries a thin, straight branch and a fatter piece of
branch about eighteen inches long*

*The two men look up at her for a moment. Mary tries to gauge the mood of the
scene in front of her. As Dylan goes back to his work, Mary feigns total
interest in the thin branch she is carrying. She places the short, thicker piece of
wood just inside the van. Her attitude and speech are softer than the night
before. She greets Dylan as one does, testing the atmosphere, after a row*

Mary Morning, Dylan.

For Frank's benefit Dylan ducks. Frank laughs

So you two chaps have found something in common after all. (*Beat*) Even
though it *is* laughing at *me*. (*To Dylan*) In the clear light of day you really
are quite a good looking boy you know. In spite of the fact that you
haven't shaved.
Dylan (*holding up his broken razor*) What do you suggest I do? Spin the
blades round on the tip of my tongue?
Mary Behold a tent pole! Would you mind holding the apex for me?
Dylan No need, we're going. Thank you very much for the thought, but . . .
Mary Yes, but you'll still need a trusty pole.

Dylan ignores her

No? Frank, come here a moment, will you.

Frank I'm fighting a bacon sandwich.

Mary It won't take two shakes of a dragon's tail. (*Beat*) That was a little ethnic joke which seems to have been wasted on you both. Wales? Dragons? (*Beat*) No.

Dylan (*looking up at Mary*) Do you know what the dragon uses his tail for?

Mary Wagging?

Dylan Killing people.

Mary Oh Frank ... we're in the presence of an expert.

A slight pause. Dylan looks at her

Dylan We most certainly are.

Mary smiles broadly and unnecessarily. She stops suddenly

Mary (*sharply*) Frank!

With a sigh Frank puts his sandwich down and holds up the tent for her. Mary puts the new pole in place and then stands back

There! Quite an acceptable compromise. Frank, dear, nip inside and put up the other one.

Frank crawls into the tent and, in his own time, erects the far pole

(*Her eyes lighting on Dylan's bin liner*) Good heavens, what a lot of rubbish you've got.

Dylan Our stuff. Will you be claiming salvage?

Mary Put it all back in the tent when Frank emerges and we'll have breakfast. (*Pause*) Where's Apricot? Still slugging abed? It's not right for a young girl ...

Dylan You are utterly *amazing*!

Mary Why do you sound surprised? I've *always* thought so. (*She re-sets the sandwiches out on picnic plates*) One for Mary, one for Apricot, one for Frank ...

Dylan (*quickly*) I've eaten, thanks ...

Mary Oh, so you like my cooking then. Hadn't someone better go for Apricot? (*Of a mug*) Frank, please don't leave teaspoons in the mugs. It's so secondary modern.

Frank (*coming out of the tent*) Mary ... Dylan and Apricot are going. It's a verb, meaning "to soon not be here".

The tent collapses

And that's called gravity.

Mary (*to Dylan*) But why?

Frank (*about to expain the law of gravity*) Well it started with an apple ...

Dylan I'm not absolutely sure, Mrs Challis ...

Mary Mary.

Dylan ... but it may have something to do with last night.

Mary Last night? (*Beat*) Yes, I do see the direction you're leading me in, but where are *you* going?

Dylan Home!

Mary And where is home?

Dylan Acton.

Mary Where the flyovers come from. I know it well. Tell me, is the A40 finished yet or still at the experimental stage? (*She sips her tea and recoils*) Frank, there's no sweetener!

Frank Sorry. (*He reaches for the dispenser and fires one into her mug*)

Mary sits down on one of the camping chairs

Mary (*very gently*) Dylan, if your mother isn't there, how can you call it home?

Dylan For a start people don't back in through the front door and mow the furniture down.

Mary And what about Apricot? She should have an equal say in the matter, you know. Mrs Pankhurst chained herself to some pretty downmarket railings to make that very point. (*She picks up the short piece of wood*) Where's my knife, Frank?

Frank In the glove compartment. (*He turns to go and get it*)

Dylan feels compelled to come in on Frank's side. He points violently at Frank as he goes to the passenger door

Dylan You see! Habit! Habit!

Mary squints into the undergrowth excitedly, hoping to see a rabbit

Mary Where? Where?

Dylan stands in front of her and exudes the soul of reason

Dylan Mrs Challis ... Mary ...

Mary (*reacting with a smile to her Christian name*) Yes, dear?

Dylan Last night is a thing of the past ...

Mary What a first rate perspective on time you have ...

Dylan ... and what you're still struggling to avoid is an apology. I say forget it and we'll be on our way.

Frank gives Mary a knife from the glove compartment. It is a small bladed thing for carving wood

Mary (*setting to work, whittling off the bark*) Last night we heard much about the stainless steel quality of Apricot's spine. Well, as Frank will confirm for us, she also has a spleen. On another occasion he can give us a lecture about its function. I expect it does something terribly important to grape pips ...

Frank (*with quiet enthusiasm*) No, that's the append ...

Mary (*shouting him down*) All I know is that it's an organ one *vents*. Apricot should have her chance to do so.

Dylan I don't think she's that petty!

Mary Nonsense, dear. We *all* are. And if the midget won't come to Mary, then Mary must go to the midget. (*She begins to get up*)

Dylan (*gesturing her not to*) I'll take her a cylinder of tea . . . see what she says.

Mary (*handing him a mug of tea*) Does she take sugar?

Dylan Two.

Mary Yes, well tell her, in passing, she should cut down on sugar. She's tiny with a round face . . . and that'll be where all the unburned calories wind up. (*She puts one spoonful of sugar into the mug and stirs*) She can start now. One spoonful . . . level.

Dylan Tell me, do you rule the world or just Aylesbury?

Mary (*lifting the flap of a sandwich*) Does she like bacon? (*Before he can answer*) Of course she does. With the rind on or off? Frank, you might have crisped the bacon!

Frank (*severely, for him*) Mary, *you* know it, *Dylan* knows it, *I* know it . . . you're terrified of what you said, so you bounced out of the van at the crack of dawn, loaded your mouth and let it blast away!

Dylan Bravo Frank!

There is a slight pause. Frank is delighted to have won Dylan's praise

Mary (*appalled*) You two boys have conspired against me. I turn my back for five seconds and get a poisoned arrow in the neck!

Frank My sympathy goes out to the arrow.

Mary (*impressed, to Dylan*) Good heavens! He's not at all witty as a rule. Now . . . (*she gets up*) . . . let me give you a plan. Take these goodies to your sister and say the following: "How would you like to be downright rude to the old bat who was cruel to you last night?" Tell her she can have two minutes of uninterrupted Anglo-Saxon.

Dylan (*smiling*) And then are we free to go?

Mary As far away as you like, dear. (*Pause*) On the other hand, you might like to consider the possibility . . .

Frank (*severely*) Mary button it!

Mary (*to Dylan; of Frank*) Dylan, you have had a bad influence on my friend. (*She takes Frank's hand*) Perhaps we *both* needed to nearly run over someone like you. (*She goes up to Dylan*) Will you accept a most unlikely possibility?

Dylan You're *not* Mary Poppins?

Mary . . . that for once in my life my brain is fully locked in to the words I'm about to say.

Frank would nudge Dylan if he were near enough to him

Frank I can hear the key turning. The lock is rusty.

With some considerable effort Mary reveals another flaw in her personality

Mary It's very difficult for me to think before I speak. I've spent forty years listening to words that just fell out of my mouth. But *you* . . . you as well as Apricot . . . must forgive me for what I said. (*Pause*) There! It's really quite easy once you get going, isn't it? Now, off you go, there's a good chap. (*She claps her hands twice*) Quickly, quickly.

Dylan feels able to trade one of his own vulnerabilities with Mary. He stares at her. She puts her hands on his shoulders and pulls him towards her ... then she kisses him on the cheek. For a moment he forgets where he is, not to mention who Mary is, closes his eyes and lets his head drop onto her shoulder ...

There is a slight pause

I've a camping sachet of hair shampoo in the van. I'll find it for you.

Dylan (*suddenly snapping out of his relapse*) What the hell am I doing! One blast on the horn we fight *there*, two, we do it *here*. Brace yourself! She's almost as dirty a fighter as you are.

He exits with the tea and the bacon sandwich

Mary (*excitedly*) Frank did you see that? The boy actually put his head on my shoulder! Like a son or something! I mean when *you* put your head on my shoulder we always bump. Can't you do anything about that?

Frank Mary, just because I'm a doctor doesn't mean I can reshape your head. Calm down, girl.

Mary A young man puts his head on my shoulder and quick as a flash you're criticizing my bone structure!

Frank Mary ... at the risk of a lecture, what you're doing is called "displacement activity". The brat who overtakes you in his Ford Capri ... what does he do? He scratches an itch he hasn't got behind his ear as if to say, "Good heavens, I've just overtaken a car."

Mary I've this overwhelming desire to scratch my left ear. (*She does so*) That's better.

Frank Young men scratch. Mary Challis rabbits ...

More in fun than seriousness Mary turns to look for the rabbit

Mary Another one? Good God, they're breeding like people. (*She calms down almost totally*) Frank ...

Frank Yes?

Mary (*turning away*) No ... it's nothing ...

Frank (*on her behalf*) "Frank, I am frightened ..."

Mary (*sharply*) Good God, why on earth should I be frightened?

Frank is going very carefully with Mary, just as an old friend should

Frank Because you're about to meet another generation head on. I believe him when he says she's a dirty fighter. Getting a pill down her throat last night was like loading a cannon.

Mary throws down the wood she has been whittling. She is appalled with herself

Mary Mary Challis, who puts the fear of God into the Aylesbury Chamber of Commerce is frightened?! She's nineteen, Frank, and only half the street fighter I am. ... (*She pauses, then accepts that she is frightened*) I've never spoken to anyone of nineteen before, not that I can remember. Not even when I was nineteen. (*Courage revived*) And I'm blaming *you* for that, Frank ...

Frank (*shrugging with a grand gesture of generosity*) But of *course* you are.

Mary's command of words is staggering. She rattles on like a word processor gone mad

Mary You've restricted my social life to Sunday sherry at the Golf Club *before* church, not *after* it, so I can't even get drunk and join in the sparkling chat about putters and fairways. The unthinkable in pursuit of the unsinkable. (*She points at his face viciously*) And *that* is your wood boring insect look, searching my soul.

Frank (*kindly*) Mary, you cannot take those children home with you ...

She has to pause for Frank has hit it on the head. She regroups for a further attack

Mary Why ever not? They'll love it there. Big garden to play in ... well I know they don't play at that age, they kind of ... waste time. So be it. Nice long walks with the Airedales, a room of their own. Each. *Two* if they want it. Rooms I haven't *seen* for twenty years. I mean in spite of the Mercedes they are definitely council house, wouldn't you say?

Frank They are seventeen and twenty.

Mary What absolute *rubbish*!

Frank is desperate by now, if only to ensure that Mary doesn't get hurt or make an irredeemable fool of herself

Frank Mary, age is one of life's *absolutes*! Even *you* can't argue it away or make it different! I tell you they're seventeen and twenty and you tell me that's rubbish! It *isn't*!

There is a slight pause. Mary still has a point to argue, however feebly

Mary Well ... we've only got their *word* for it ... (*her voice tails off because she knows how absurd she's being*)

Frank steels himself to say what he knows will hurt her

Frank They are adults and they will find it very hard to become the children you never had.

Mary You never lose an opportunity to remind me, do you! (*In an immediate apology, she bumps heads with him*) Or prop me up when I need it.

Frank Because you knock someone's tent over doesn't mean you have to adopt them. You don't even *know* them.

But Mary is excited in that vulnerable way of all people on a hiding to nowhere

Mary But I've got all day to put that right!

Frank You cannot buy a family ready made ... from stock. They're not *like* bookends. They live, they breathe, they move!

Mary Oh well, we can't have that, can we? (*She points wildly*) Apricot, stand
still. I will not have you photosynthesizing in the house. It makes your
leaves drop ...
Frank And they may have plans for the future that we know nothing about!
Mary (*pointing wildly*) Dylan, do not write pop songs on the walls!

Frank laughs

Dear Frank, who always tries to take the pleasure out of everything, even
dreaming. Even *I* know there will have to be compromise. (*Beat*) For a
few days.
Frank And what if they say, "Go to hell!"?
Mary They *won't* and you will live to thank me for getting two new patients
on to your panel. (*She fumbles with Dylan's cigarette packet and eventually
manages to light one*)
Frank You've got plans to make them ill already? (*Pause*) Mary ... twelve
hours ago you'd never *met* them. Now anyone'd think *you* were respon-
sible for their mother's death.
Mary I know you pride yourself on having read *one* psychology text book.
What a pity you didn't finish it!
Frank (*shaking her gently*) All I care about is that you don't get *hurt*!

Mary goes to her holdall and takes out the vodka and pours herself a measure

Mary If that was true you'd persuade them I'm not half as bad as I seem.
(*With a sudden fear*) Is half as bad as me good enough? Yes! But of course
to do that you'd have to believe it yourself, wouldn't you? (*Beat. She
closes her eyes*) And so would I. (*Anxiously*) What's keeping them?!
Where *are* they?
Frank It'll be the tea. No sugar. I mean, for God's sake, you've already
changed the poor kid's *diet*.

Mary sips her drink and smokes her cigarette

Be careful which one you swallow.
Mary And now you're giving up on me. I see. You spend a whole year of
my life telling me not to poison my body then, come the first hiccup,
you're pushing me over the edge!
Frank Did you ever wonder why I want you alive?
Mary As a matter of fact I did. And you certainly don't come out of it on a
white charger. Free meals, sex and someone to shout at.
Frank You're the worst cook I ever *met*! And as for bullying, well, any fool
can see my footprints all over you. Size ten.
Mary (*smiling at him*) There was a *third* thing, Frank. The trees and I and
all the little fauna are waiting for your comments on it.
Frank (*looking at his watch*) I'm a doctor!

Far off stage a car hoots once. Mary grabs Frank

Mary Oh God ... hold my hand, Frank! I can't go up there alone! Come
with me!

There is a longish pause before the car hoots a second time. Mary flares

He did that on purpose! A deliberate space between hoots to unnerve me!

Frank Calm down, girl. Think "Valium".

Mary (*changing gear and starting to prepare*) Right! They're coming here! Let go of me please. (*Beat*) You're better at this sort of thing than I am. People are *always* being rude to you. How do you stop yourself tying their earlobes together?

Frank (*quietly*) I love you.

Mary Don't play the fool now. Just promise to give me the nod if I start ripping into her. I think a casual, grown-up approach is what I need, don't you? (*She sits in one of the chairs*) "Good morning, Apricot. How are you this morning? (*Beat*) Dear." (*To Frank*) The odd "dear" won't sound too fulsome, will it? "You have two minutes to get me off your chest. Dear."

Frank Dylan said I *didn't* love you. I was just terrified to push you to one side.

Mary Yes, he's definitely the brighter of the two.

Frank Bright but wrong.

Mary (*with her eye on the entrance*) Frank, for once in your life, will you stop being selfish and think of others. Here am I about to offer two orphans the chance . . .

There is slight pause. Mary has at last heard what he said, and it amazes rather than flatters her

Mary You? Love me?

Frank (*nodding*) On a good day.

Mary What on earth for?

Frank That's the question I ask on the *bad* days.

Mary Why the hell choose now to tell me? You've had twenty years, but oh no, you wait till a human gunboat is about to blow my head off! (*Pause*) Unless this is pure displacement activity. Very clever. Yet you aren't clever . . . well you are, but not with people. Or even me (*Beat*) You love me?

Frank (*casually*) Yes . . .

Mary (*with pleasure*) Say it again.

Frank Nope.

Mary Ah, so you don't love me *emphatically*. Just the once. Tell me . . . do you know if I love you? I mean I've quite forgotten. I really should keep a diary and write these things down.

Apricot enters with Dylan

(*With cautious bonhomie*) Ah Apricot. Good morning. Dear. How are you? I mean you look terrible but. . . . (*She buries her face in her hand*) . . . Oh God . . .

Apricot The tea, Mrs Challis, was disgusting!

Mary Well, I'll make you some more. (*She gets up*)

Apricot No thanks.

Mary Well I won't then. (*She sits down*)

Apricot sits in the other chair and studies her

Well then . . . two minutes and counting. Off you go. (*Pause*) Apricot, I'm only counting in my head you know. . . . You'll get nothing said lolling about in a chair. Take it from one who has mixed it with vipers, Apricot. Hatred will come more readily on your feet. Why *is* that, Frank?

Frank shrugs

When it really comes down to it he knows nothing! Apricot, allow me to demonstrate the point. (*She stands up*) You be me and I'll be you . . . and you can take over at a convenient pause for breath. Right. Apricot!

Apricot Yeah?

Mary No . . . Mary, sorry. Mary, my name is Apricot, and I have stormed into this clearing to set about you with one or two home truths. First, but not necessarily foremost, Mary, you are just about one of the most . . . (*She pauses. She's baffled*) I can't (*She sits down again*)

Apricot No . . . nor can I.

Mary Well in my case there's a reason, but you should be livid! (*Pause*) Oh God, Frank, she's sorry for me.

Apricot It is, after all, only a tent.

Mary True.

There is a slight pause

Apricot And a leather jacket, a razor, vodka . . .

Mary But the things I *said*!

Apricot You look different. To what I remember . . .

Mary A whole night has passed. I've improved with age.

Apricot (*shaking her head*) Frustrated and desperate.

Mary (*rising*) My God, the cheek of it! (*To Frank and Dylan*) You two. Why don't you take yourselves to the nearest petrol pump and get this silly van moving! Frank you are . . .

Frank (*nodding as he interrupts*) . . . entirely to blame for all this? Dylan, would you be kind enough to take me to the nearest village so that we can buy some petrol . . . ?

Mary Frank, you said that politely to show me up! Well thanks! (*Sweetly*) Dylan, would you be kind enough to take my extremely rude friend to the nearest village to buy petrol so that we can get this heap out of your life?! (*She kicks the van and winces*) And you'd better leave a plaster.

Dylan Well . . . (*he looks at Apricot*)

Apricot (*to Dylan*) I'll be fine.

Mary She'll be fine! And if it's of any interest to anyone, so shall I.

Frank I think we all kind of guessed.

Mary And what is that supposed to mean?

Frank It means that I've found the petrol can and I'm off. Come on, Dylan.

Dylan Be all right without a referee, girls?

Mary Don't you patronize me, young man! Llyn Cwm Bychan is a mere stone's throw away. And you are but a pebble.

Frank exits with the petrol can, followed by Dylan

Right. Where was I?

Apricot Frustrated and desperate.

Mary You can say *that* again. . . . (*She realizes that's where they were in the conversation*) Ah yes. Well this is how it's done from cold, Apricot! How dare you presume to stroll in here, calm as a miniature mill pond and comment upon the hormonal rage within my body? I think you should confine your comments to *my* comments about your late mother! (*She stops. She softens to human*) I can't . . . I really can't, not even to you who've given me cause.

Apricot So nattering on *isn't* your only pastime.

Mary As a matter of fact, I'm a very keen gardener. . . . (*Beat*) Oh, you're being ironic. I see. The language of insult has changed over the years.

Apricot No . . . I'm genuinely curious . . .

Mary Oh that's very healthy at your age. (*Beat*) What about?

Apricot Why life for you is a game of Scrabble. I mean all I've got to do is punch a button and you'll spout forever.

Mary Displacement activity, dear. . . . Imagine, if you will, a young man in a Ford Capri . . .

Apricot You're doing it now.

Mary So I am. Shall we drink instead? Or have you things to say?

Apricot I'll yell at you, Mrs Challis, if you promise me one thing.

Mary Anything. Just ask.

Apricot Will you bring her back to life?

Mary (*smiling*) No, dear, that's a little beyond my . . . (*she stops*) I see. I answer your words but not your meaning. Yes . . . what a lot of things I'm learning today and its only nine o'clock. A man has already said he loves me, and I have nearly finished your vodka (*Beat. She smiles*) One should always try to keep busy. (*She scrutinizes Apricot*) I might see things another way. Perhaps you don't have the words or the courage to blast me off the face of the earth.

Apricot Believe me I have. I could call you a . . . well . . . a dried up, barren old tart who was maybe married for a whole week because that's all he could stand of you. But that week taught you all you needed to know about sharing your life and you didn't like it. (*She smiles*) But why should I tell you that? You know it already.

Mary (*retreating into herself*) No . . . you've got it all wrong. I wanted some children . . . really I did, but my husband died, you see. Yes, I know I made a classic mistake. I turned back onto my career. If I'd have had someone of forty-five looking over me then I'd have done things differently. But do go on.

Apricot (*shrugging*) All the talk in the world, rude or polite doesn't alter a thing. You're the best example I've met of that. I'd bet money that you're the same up here . . . (*she taps her head*) . . . as the day your old man died.

Mary Maybe. Promise me one thing. You won't take it out on your brother.

Apricot That's what brothers are for. You got any brothers?

Mary Er . . . no.

Apricot It really does show . . . that you're all alone.

Mary I didn't think it was that obvious. At any rate, I've never complained.

Apricot You should've done. Somebody, somewhere, would've listened. But you didn't think there was anything to complain *about*.

Mary Maybe I did then; can't remember; I don't now. Just because your mother's dead, Apricot, doesn't mean you're the only person in the world who understands the meaning of loss.

Apricot (*laughing*) Loss? What loss? (*Beat. Quietly*) I didn't really like her that much.

Mary (*slightly shocked*) Oh no, dear, you *did*! Everyone likes their mother!

Apricot Do you lose everything in translation, Mary? Or only what you don't want to hear? (*Beat*) She wasn't too keen on me either. She liked Dylan, of course, because everyone does. He was the husband she never had and I was the competition. . . .

Mary Then why all this fuss? Me, padding around all night, feeling guilty . . .

Apricot . . . I spent my whole life trying to make her my best friend. Now I'm stranded. Just like you. Wondering what to do next.

Mary Except that I've got a *hell* of a start on you. One I could do without. (*Beat*) How would you like a *new* mother? (*And it's asked as if it's only an academic question*) A brand new gleaming one? (*Beat*) Well, not exactly gleaming . . .

Apricot Gillian Bartlett was enough.

We hear a car, far off, start and move, coming nearer to us

Mary is disappointed by Apricot's academic answer

Mary Oh! (*She brightens up*) Then let's have a drink instead. I must have a drink.

Apricot (*picking up the bottle*) Not much left.

Mary Oh, I don't mean that cheap old supermarket rubbish. I mean . . . (*she smiles and points up at the branches above her*) . . . a gift from above. Whisky? A young girl should know how to drink.

Apricot I was learning. Till somebody stole my practice bottle.

Mary goes upstage to a tree and from behind it she shows Apricot a loop of string. It has been slung over the branch she pointed up at and attached to the other end is a bottle of scotch in a string shopping bag. Mary busies herself untying the knot

Mary We may have more in common than you think, Apricot. Yes, indeed, I've shelved my life too, you know. Well, of course you know. It takes someone like you to see it. But I'd gone further. I was in the process of boxing it up ready for storage in the loft. (*She lowers the bottle*)

Apricot is silently bewildered at this elaborate device for getting a drink. The bottle stops, six feet above the ground. Mary re-ties the knot. Apricot tries to reach up to the bottle but is too short. Mary towers over her, smiles down at her, reaches up and takes the bottle from the shopping bag

Apricot (*with genuine bewilderment*) Why up there?
Mary Because it's the last place he'd dream of looking. His neck's too fat. His head's too heavy. He just can't manage it.

A car is heard, stopping

Oh my God! It's stopped! (*She gives Apricot the bottle*) Quickly! Take it!
Apricot (*taking it, cautiously*) You mean you're *scared* of him?
Mary In a way. (*Beat*) But don't ever tell him I said so.

A car door opens and is slammed shut

A few moments later Dylan enters nervously

Apricot hides the bottle behind her back

Dylan (*eventually*) I'm not quite sure how to put this ... but ... well ... Frank's in a bit of a state.
Mary Always is, dear. Thinks he's the only man in the world who can drive.
Dylan Yes ... it's a bit *more* than that this time. ... (*He glances back, off, to where he left Frank in his car. Bravely he perseveres with the task Frank has entrusted to him*) I said to him ... Well ..., "Go and ask her yourself!" He kind of started to twitch again. I've never seen a doctor quake before. So I tried to tell him, "She can't be that bad!"
Mary To which he replied, "Oh yes she can."
Dylan (*quickly*) But I'm sure he didn't *mean* it.

Mary nods her assurance that he did mean it

Mary So what's his latest beef?
Dylan He wants to know if you'll ...
Mary Whatever it is I *won't*!
Dylan ... marry him.
Mary (*with a reflex response*) What the hell for?
Dylan Stay there a tick. I'll go back and ask ... (*he turns to exit*)
Mary (*preventing him*) No don't! Dylan, do you think he *means* it?
Dylan Yes, he does.
Mary Oh dear. Well, can you tell him to give me say ... twenty minutes to come up with a reasonable excuse ... (*she corrects herself quickly*) ... answer.
Dylan Right.

Dylan smiles and exits quickly the way he came in

A few moments later the car engine fires and is driven away

Mary and Apricot settle down individually, presumably to ask themselves if the proposal they've both heard was real

Mary pours herself a double measure of whisky into a flask top. Eventually she speaks quite casually

Mary Did a young man just hurtle into the clearing and ask me to marry an older man?

Apricot Yeah!

Mary (*very pleased*) What a busy day we're all having.

CURTAIN

ACT II

Scene 1

The same, twenty minutes later

When the Curtain *rises Mary and Apricot are breaking into the bottle of whisky for perhaps the second time*

Mary sits carving a wooden love spoon

Apricot is putting on make-up beside her

Apricot So, are you going to marry him?
Mary Depends on a couple of things, actually.
Apricot (*of the spoon*) What's that going to be?
Mary (*of the carving*) What does it look like?
Apricot A spoon.
Mary Thank God for that! A *love* spoon. Very Welsh.
Apricot You look as if you've carved things up before.
Mary It's my trade. Cabinet maker ... like the Prime Minister. Only mine last longer.
Apricot So what else do you make? Apart from things to stir with.
Mary Disgracefully expensive oak tables, dressers, chairs ... anything. People travel miles just to buy a Mary Challis.
Apricot Why are you chucking it then?
Mary Because at my age ... forty-one ...
Apricot You were forty-two yesterday.
Mary Doesn't time fly. Back and forth. At my age the only pleasure I get is from beating table tops to make them look older than me, or swiping them with the old machette. Sword cuts, you know. Why did our forefathers always fight over dinner? Must've been the cooking. (*Beat*) But who am I doing it for? Me? The dogs? The tax man? So I said "To hell with it!" Wales and hell have much in common. (*She nods out* L) Is the lake still there?
Apricot Can't say I really noticed. Other things on my mind.
Mary (*nodding*) Gillian Bartlett ...
Apricot I didn't *hate* her you know ...
Mary I understand. I've been thinking too, between sips and chips. My mother was something of a mixed blessing. Doesn't stop me missing the old boot. But I wouldn't have chosen her, given the choice.

There is a slight pause

Apricot She was the wettest female I've *ever* known!

Mary Then let me say that you don't take after her.

Apricot A lazy cow! Never out of bed till ten, never dressed till twelve!

Mary How did you manage? As children?

Apricot I became mother to them both.

Mary You make it sound so easy.

Apricot Ran the house, cooked the meals, washed and ironed and some-where in the middle of that I went to school.

Mary Was she always a ... well ... a drippy Daphne?

Apricot No. There was a time when she hated my guts ...

Mary I hardly think that's the opposite of drippy.

Apricot ... not Dylan ... just me. (*Beat*) God knows who knocked the stuffing out of her. (*Beat*) Maybe *I* did.

Mary You say that just to feel nice and guilty.

Apricot She was such a drip that she died of it.

There is a slight pause

Mary What do you mean?

Apricot She must have been ill for years. Never did a thing about it. Then in the space of two months ... (*she snaps her fingers*) ... out like a light.

Mary puts her carving aside and turns purposefully to Apricot

Mary Right! So *you* feel guilty about it. Last night *I* did. We're both wrong ... yes, even me. (*Beat*) You can be blamed for what you *did*, but not for what your mother *didn't*. (*To herself*) Does that make any sense what-soever? (*She smiles*) Good God, I believe it does

Apricot So if she'd been yours, how would you remember her?

Mary (*smiling*) As someone *desperately* in need of a plumber. (*Beat. She answers seriously*) Mathematically. I'd subtract everything I didn't like about her from everything I did. I guarantee you'll wind up with a human being. (*She picks up her carving*) It works in Frank's case. (*Beat*) Just about.

Apricot (*laughing*) Why do you pretend not to like him?

Mary Insurance, dear. Against the possibility of having chosen a real ... well ...

Apricot Drip?

Mary (*smiling*) Yes. But I have to tell you they're all the same. Lovers, fathers ... mothers, husbands.

Apricot But they don't *have* to be!

Mary Indeed they don't. Tell me, why is Dylan rich?

Apricot Well, when you spend the first ten years of your life at the top of a Walthamstow high rise you've got two choices. Throw yourself over the balcony or get lucky.

Mary And since you believe Dylan has wings, hurling himself over the edge wouldn't have worked.

Apricot Oh don't get me wrong. I don't think he's absolutely wonderful.

Mary But he is "Something else" as we used to say. All those years ago.

Apricot Now we still *say* that, funnily enough.

Mary What exactly *is* he?

Apricot A middle man. That boy will buy up anything and keep it tucked away for a rainy day. Then bang! At the right moment he flogs it off at a huge mark-up. His last coup was two hundred acres of runner beans.

Mary In Walthamstow? Two hundred acres?

Apricot (*laughing*) Cambridgeshire.

Mary But where did he keep them?

Apricot Well that's where he really comes into his own. He bought a warehouse too. Come the day someone needs a warehouse he'll flog that off as well.

Mary (*cautiously*) He's not a ... crook, is he?

Apricot (*smiling at the quaint word*) More *secretive* really. One of those people who can peel an orange in their pockets.

Mary (*forgetting where she is*) Only I won't have a crook in the house!

Apricot That's why you're short of friends.

Mary No ... he can't be a crook. He's looked after his sister. (*Beat*) Where *are* those men? I use the term loosely.

Apricot (*smiling*) They've run out of diesel.

Mary What are *your* plans, Apricot?

Apricot Don't know any more. I was doing A levels when Mum died.

Mary Will I sound too much like her if I say there's plenty of time?

Apricot I'm nearly eighteen for God's sake!

Mary Yes, yes, of course. You must be careful not to let life slip by on the inside.

Apricot I'll get myself cranked up soon, I suppose. Apply to UCCA.

Mary Is that a planet or a virus?

Apricot University clearing house. And I'll wind up taking second best. As always.

Mary (*sharply*) No you won't! (*She stops herself playing mother*) Or rather you mustn't ... needn't ... I mean please don't. (*Beat*) You have my word that you'll regret it.

Apricot What was he *like*?

Mary My husband?

Apricot nods

Second best. A perfect example of prehistoric man. Utterly invertebrate.

Apricot So who was first?

Mary (*pausing, then risking the confidence*) He's on the road with your brother, somewhere between here and a petrol pump. (*Beat*) But don't ever tell him that, will you?

Apricot You going to marry him?

Mary (*smiling*) It depends on a couple of things really. (*She tightens*) Plus Frank's daughter, Jennifer. A mean runner bean of a girl who rules his life. (*Beat*) We should get Dylan to buy her up and flog her. Extremely hard.

Apricot What happened to his wife?

Mary She died soon after they were married. Which is why Frank is such a gentle creature, I suppose. He's frightened I'll go any day now. (*She*

begins to lift the mood) He says that as I slip along the rollers *en route* to
the rose garden, via the flames of Aylesbury Crematorium, my coffin will
open, just a few inches, a hand will emerge . . . (*she acts it out*) . . . thus . . .
tap the ash off a Gauloise, and retreat. (*She mimes the coffin lid shutting
tight*) Snap!

Apricot Kick your bad habits, Mary. He may not fancy the idea of
marrying a rose bush.

Mary Oh he's *immensely* adaptable.

Apricot Tough old bird like you could jump on the wagon tomorrow.

Mary Well, dear, in spite of the way you put it, I'll take that as a
compliment. But what does it leave Frank with?

Apricot Perrier water.

A car is heard in the distance, approaching the clearing

Mary (*sadly*) What I *mean* is, am I the sum total of everything I've drunk in
the last ten years? Is every word I've said, every thought I've had, firmly
based on grape and grain?

Apricot You make it all sound so *feeble*! Just look at you! Running away
from a biddy little town to an even biddier little country.

The car stops, off

Mary Why does it seem to bother you?

Apricot Because I've just subtracted what I didn't like about someone from
what I *do*.

*Dylan stomps on to the stage, carrying two packages, a newspaper and the
petrol can. He slams the packages down in the van one by one*

Dylan That's for lunch! That's for supper! (*He puts the can down*) That's for
the van! Had a good fight?

Mary (*coming over to him*) Most productive.

Dylan (*nodding*) Smells like it.

Mary (*turning away*) What have you done with Frank?

Dylan (*obviously fed up with Frank*) Frank has lockjaw . . . (*he counts the
ailments off on his fingers*) . . . hypertension, dyspepsia, depression,
shingles and his whole body is locked hard and fast in the shape of a
butcher's hook. (*Beat*) Personally, I think he's ill.

Mary (*smiling maternally*) And how are *you*, Dylan?

Dylan I am what you call fine! But if you don't say you'll marry him I will
kill all three of you! Does that sound fair?

Mary (*eventually, quietly*) Very. So . . . yes.

Dylan An extremely wise move!

He stomps off R

Mary (*quietly*) Or did I mean no?

Dylan (*off, calling*) Come on, Frank . . . she said yes.

Dylan enters, sits on a rock and reads the paper

Frank enters casually and calmly, his hysteria all behind him in the Mercedes

Mary inclines her head towards Frank, expecting, at the very least, a peck on the cheek. Frank heads for the van, totally ignoring her. Pause. He notices the silence, looks at Mary and worries

Frank What's wrong with your neck?
Mary (*sighing and retracting her neck*) It's not long enough to reach you, Frank.
Frank Any coffee?
Mary Are we seeing you at your most romantic or if we hang about will you rush me into the trees and shake my hand? Passionately!
Frank Mary, all we've done is agree on a practical means of . . . making the rest of our lives bearable.
Mary For you, I suppose, that is passionate.

Frank flops down, exhausted probably, in the other chair. Dylan lowers the paper and stares at Frank

Dylan Ten minutes ago, Frank, you were planning a trip to the North Pole if she turned you down. (*Beat*) Alone.
Frank Well, she didn't. You were right. I was wrong. Why are you all on at me?
Apricot (*over to Frank*) I think she'd like a sort of public statement. Along the lines of, "I love you".
Frank Well, she can't have it!
Apricot (*to Frank*) Doesn't it deserve even one kiss?
Frank (*looking at Mary*) My lips won't stretch that far. Can I have the sports page, Dylan?
Dylan No.
Mary Very well, Frank, if it's practicality you want you shall have it. We'll live at my house.
Frank I thought we'd always agreed that mine was nicer.
Mary But small.
Frank Very well. Your house.
Mary Why do you give in so easily?
Frank (*sighing*) All right. (*By rote*) Oh no, Mary, I don't want to live in your house. It's too big. Oh very well if you insist. Your house. (*Beat*) Was that better?
Mary No, it was rude.
Frank It doesn't matter a damn where we live. As long as it's not in Wales.
Mary There's no need to get patriotic, Frank. The long day's journey into this Godforsaken wilderness was only a cry from the heart.
Frank Good. I still think my house is nicer.
Mary Why are you being so difficult? Your house is full of old beams which is fine for you, but I keep whacking my head on them. It'd be fine for Apricot. If and when you ever grow into a size twelve, Frank, you'll know how it feels to duck ten times on a journey from your living room to the

kitchen. (*She bobs her head up and down*) It's cork in a stormy sea time!
(*And if she malaprops the line, so much the better*)
Frank If you laid off the booze you'd see the beams coming ...
Apricot (*nervously*) Your first row.
Frank ... but since you won't, get yourself a crash helmet!

*Dylan wrestles the paper away from his face, bangs out the rhythm of his
speech on the arm of the chair, angry for the first time since we met him*

Dylan You will go to live in *Mary's house!* (*Beat. He apologizes*) I'm sorry.
(*He goes back to the paper*)
Mary That's settled then. And Dylan can have the room over the conserva-
tory.
Dylan (*behind the paper*) Thanks.

And Mary's mouth has slipped its leash again

Mary Oh you'll love it, Dylan. It has a phone extension, you see ... very
essential to the rise and rise of a runner bean baron. Apricot, the west
wing for you, I think ...
Frank (*rising from his chair*) Mary ...

*Mary pushes him down. Dylan's paper slowly lowers as he listens. In his own
time he will fold it incredibly neatly as Mary rattles on. Apricot is as
bewildered as her brother by Mary's assumptions*

Mary I say the west wing, dear, because you'll need some peace and quiet.
We'll get that very sniffy designer in from Amersham. (*Impatient with
herself*) Oh Frank, what the devil's his name? (*To Dylan*) I'm awful with
names.
Frank Apparently. His name is Elaine.
Mary Well she dresses in baggy jeans and a tie; you know the sort? Hair cut
right back to the follicles. Have you got a good *desk*, Apricot? Without a
good desk how is a girl to take the academic world by storm?
Dylan (*slightly scared now*) What the hell are you talking about?
Mary (*as if it's a sensible answer to Dylan's question*) The swimming pool
and the tennis court. They are in a sorry state. No, Frank, I'm not
blaming you, though you're the only one who uses them. (*She laughs at
her next thought*) They'll have to come to terms with Mr and Mrs
Peterson, won't they Frank? She's shorter than you, Apricot and shrink-
ing all the time I understand. One morning soon, over breakfast, I'm
bound to peel her head and stick a soldier in it. But ... (*she holds up a
warning finger*) ... where the croquet mallets are concerned, she is
unmerciful. Leave one out overnight at your peril. Dylan, there's a whole
range of garages for your Mercedes and your beans. Do you like dogs? Of
course you do. But do you like cats? I have two, though for the life of me I
can't remember their names ...
Frank Eric and Brian.
Mary I would ask only one thing. Sadly, we're not on mains drainage so
don't go bunging old socks down the toilets ... of which there are four.
Or is it three? Anyway, there's enough. And on the subject of toilets I

should mention the rockery. (*A puzzled look comes over her face but not at the expense of keeping talking*) I'm not quite sure why, but I know I should. Ah yes. It's because I buy my plants from a nursery in Twyford. If you see a cat digging around in it shout, "Biscuits!" Now, why should the word "Biscuits" terrify a cat, I hear you ask. Well, it doesn't. But the dogs will appear from nowhere and, cats being cats, will run away from a dog hell bent on a biscuit. Any questions?

There is a pause

Dylan Only one. What the hell are you talking about?

Mary (*smiling*) Do you really want me to say it all again? I *could* you know ...

Dylan (*in genuine disbelief*) You mean you want us to. ... (*He laughs at the preposterous notion*) No. ...

Mary You tell them, Frank.

Frank No.

Mary Apricot? Well this is a fine start, I must say! Nobody wants to talk to each other. All I'm saying is that you must come and live with me. And you must as well, Frank ... don't feel left out.

Dylan (*eventually*) Ah ...

Mary So when shall we leave? Tomorrow morning?

Dylan I think we'll just mosey off now. Come on, Ape.

Mary But you don't know where it is!

Dylan It's in Aylesbury.

Mary Oh good grief, no! Not *in* Aylesbury. *Near* Aylesbury. Where's the atlas, Frank?

Dylan moves to the tent and starts to pick up things which lie around outside it

Frank Mary, I think what Dylan would like to say is, "Thanks but no thanks".

Mary (*moving to Dylan and tapping him on the shoulder*) You'll be pleased to know that we're not on the Milton Keynes side of Aylesbury. We're on the Oxford side ... (*she turns*) ... a fact that should spur you on to great things, Apricot. We have an apricot espalier on the south wall you know. Isn't that strange? Well, it isn't really because we've also got a peach, a plum and a Worcester apple. (*Beat*) You're not going to tell me at this late stage that you hate fruit. ...

Dylan (*trying to be kind*) Mary ... how can I best put this. ...

Mary You *loathe* it! We shall tear them all down and plant roses.

Dylan We ... er ... don't ...

Mary Yes?

Dylan Well ... we *can't!*

His gesture of desperation halts Mary for a good few moments. She steps off her insane high and calms almost to sanity level

Mary No ... of course you can't.

Dylan (*to Apricot*) Come on, kid ... let's pack.

Mary (*to Frank only*) Was it something I said, maybe?

Frank (*taking her hand*) I warned you.

Mary Why did you plan on marrying me if it wasn't for them?

Frank I told you. Love.

And that reply halts Mary

Mary Oh I see. (*She turns to Dylan and Apricot haughtily*) Really ... one would not have expected the young to be so ungrateful. Or unkind. Or stupid.

Dylan Keep going Mary. You'll win us over.

Mary Or sarcastic. We meet by chance in a far off glade which turns out to be a centre of gravity for us all. Me with no family, you with no mother, and with Frank to referee. And you won't seize the opportunity with both hands! Are you frightened?

Dylan Not at all.

Mary Then think of *me*. Dylan, please put the tent down. (*He doesn't*) I said please put ...

Dylan is clear in his mind but anxious and determined to put Mary straight

Dylan I hear what you said! "Think of *me*." It's what you've said all your life! And you'll go on saying it till the day you die. (*He softens*) Thank you all the same. We don't want your home. We have one ... and friends.

Mary (*with a slight relapse*) They can come and stay!

Dylan We are eighteen and twenty-one.

Mary Not till next birthday.

Dylan We're not orphans in a storm ...

Mary But it could be such *fun*, don't you see ... ?

Dylan No! You see us out on the lawn, dressed in sailor suits, cast-iron furniture all around, big pots of lemonade and home-made cakes! Cold winter evenings, sat round a wireless sipping Ovaltine before bed at nine! (*Beat*) You're also pissed as a rat.

Mary I'll stop drinking, I swear it, if you stop the swearing!

Dylan You've told us what we can do for *you*. We can make a foursome for tennis ... *if* we let you win, I suppose. We can fill your house, quietly, cleanly, respectfully. We can play in your garden, as long as we don't walk on the flower beds or throw stones at the conservatory. (*Gently*) We can take you back in time to what you should have had. If life was fair. But life *ain't* fair!

Mary (*correcting his English before she can stop herself*) Isn't fair.

Dylan (*smiling kindly*) And no doubt you'll teach us to talk proper. Life isn't fair. Each one of us here knows that for sure. But it's no reason to form a club. (*A slight pause*) What you haven't said ... what you didn't even think was necessary ... is what *you* will give *us*.

Mary I told you. A home.

Dylan And I told you back that we've got one.

Apricot pipes up very firmly, insistent upon making her presence felt

Apricot (*to Dylan*) Which *I* don't want to see again!

Mary Fantastic! One down, one to go!

Dylan Mary, we are not two green bottles, sitting on a wall!

Mary There speaks a natural born gin drinker.

Dylan And everything does not come down to a double measure on the rocks. Come on Ape. (*He motions her to join him with the packing*)

Apricot No!

Dylan They're casting around for things to do with the rest of their lives!

Apricot And what the hell do you think *I'm* doing? Exactly the same! And you should be too, unless you plan on driving round Wales for the next fifty years!

Dylan If you don't get a written agreement she'll kick you out within a month.

Apricot You understand vegetables so well. Why don't you recognize a good deal when it comes to people?

Dylan Because she's a *selfish* cow, that's why!

Mary (*sweetly*) Isn't that strange? I can't see it myself.

Dylan It's taken you twenty years to get round to marrying *him*. Even then it took me, a complete stranger, to *throw* him at you! Why would you suddenly change? All you want is the same life with more objects in the background to talk about. (*He impersonates her*) "Yesterday, my dears, I picked up an absolute bargain. A brace of children! One of each variety. Plucked! Trussed! And dressed!"

There is a slight pause

Mary Frank, hit him!

Frank Why should I? He does you very well.

Dylan And you're as bad as her, only smarter.

Mary (*narked*) Well! I'm prepared to admit that he's rotten to the core, but cleverer?

Frank No, hang on Mary. (*To Dylan*) I'd like to hear your opinion of me.

Dylan She appeals to your bloated sense of self sacrifice. "Look what I tried to do for her," you'll say at her funeral. "If only she'd listened to me . . . she'd be with us today. I tried . . . God knows I tried . . . Where's my medal?"

Mary Do you have a date for my demise, Dylan? If you have, I think I should be the first to know. Is it worth pricking out the winter cabbage for example?

Dylan Who'll take her place, Frank? Some other cripple?

Frank Dylan, you're a treat. A view as black as yours is bound to make you a million. No friends, but a million.

Dylan (*shrugging*) So I see people for what they are.

Frank (*not pleased but staying calm*) When I set out for Wales, from Aylesbury, all those centuries ago, I expected to pass a few people on the road, but I never expected to meet God. How nice to make your acquaintance.

Dylan Come on, Frank, she's your left arm. But the pair of you have spent twenty years afraid to pick each other up, scared to put each other down. Dog and flea, changing roles depending on whose turn it is to suck blood.

Mary (*to Frank*) Were we ever that self-righteous?

Frank Oh yes.

Mary He means no! Apricot, the offer still stands! It isn't quite the way I planned it but one must always be ready with a sturdy compromise ...

Frank (*cautioning*) Mary ...

Mary (*still to Apricot*) You and I will get on famously. Let me know your decision by lunch time. I refuse to be messed around.

Apricot (*in a small voice*) Lunch time it is then.

Mary (*appalled*) You mean you don't know now?

Apricot (*in an even smaller voice*) You said lunch ...

Dylan Lady's in a hurry to wipe out her past, Ape.

Apricot exits

Mary (*yelling after her*) Lunch is at twelve!

Frank You know something, Dylan? You could be right.

Mary For God's sake don't mope, Frank. How can he be right at twenty?

Frank Though I never saw myself as a flea, I must admit.

Dylan So you live and learn, even at your great age.

Mary What is it Dylan? Can't you wait to turn her against us?

Dylan You're doing the job *for* me. Beautifully.

Mary You obviously didn't reckon on doing battle with Mary Challis.

Frank All of a sudden it's a war? I thought you wanted to take them home with us.

Mary It would have been nice, I admit. But I will not be told *what* I am and *why* by a council house yob from Acton out of Walthamstow!

Dylan Now I'm a racehorse.

Mary And I will *not* have you skulking round my house summing me up ...

Frank (*to Dylan*) Especially so well.

Mary Quiet, Frank! Dear. You don't like me being honest. It's fine for you to call me selfish ... accuse me of having nothing useful to do with my time.

Dylan Well have you?

Mary Of course. Did you never hear of ... well ... reading and bonsai and reading *about* bonsai?

Dylan (*beat*) Why are you scared of being soft?

Mary People walk all over you.

Dylan Rubbish! *Some* people walk over you, not all!

Mary The others cower in a corner.

Dylan So why did Ape suddenly get to like you?

Mary She's a woman. They're different from men.

Frank Mary! Your mind is clearing, allowing second-hand thoughts to enter.

Mary I let her say her piece, nothing more.

Frank You let her talk? Good God, we want to know what was said.

Mary Are you marking me out of ten? If so, I shall probably have to help you with the counting.

Frank You found you weren't afraid of her, didn't you? But Dylan, he's a different thing altogether.

Mary I've been most polite to Dylan, maternal even.

Frank He scares the living hell out of you. But tell me something, did you ever stop to think about us while trading your refined insults with him?

Mary Us?

Frank You and me, you daft bitch. Half an hour ago we planned on spending the next twenty years together.

Mary What's that got to do with anything?

Frank It's got something to do with me. Door mat, punchbag, and ... referee. Remember? The one who keeps trying to save your life? Do I fit into this domestic jigsaw you're piecing together?

Mary Oh yes, Frank, of course you'll have a place in the new arrangements. Which room do you want?

Frank I rather fancied sharing one with you. After all, I don't need peace and quiet. But I wasn't talking about rooms.

Mary I know. You want to keep me all to yourself ... away from them. No wonder they call it a nuclear family, it's always on the verge of destruction.

Frank I just wondered, in the much-maligned spirit of self-interest, what was to become of me?

Mary Are all fathers so selfish? Me, me, me! That's all we ever hear from you!

Frank I also wondered what we'll do when all the dust has settled. Do you and I rock on in the same old way? Afraid to pick each other up, scared to put each other down?

Mary Those are words, just words. Put into the head of a young man with no feelings for people!

Frank A young man whose mother died eight weeks ago.

Mary Yes ... I know.

Dylan If this is what people call domestic bliss, I think I'll pass on it.

Mary Where are you going?

Dylan I take it I'm free to disappear?

Mary Certainly. If you go now, you'll spend the next ten years wondering what you've missed.

Dylan Trapped by all that you've got to offer?

Mary That's right!

Dylan exits

He wasn't meant to do that! Why will nobody do what I tell them? Frank ... you are entirely to ... (*she stops herself*)

Frank Perhaps he needed twenty minutes to come up with a reasonable excuse ... answer.

Frank takes hold of Mary to comfort her. Their heads bump

CURTAIN

SCENE 2

The same, about half an hour later

When the CURTAIN *rises Dylan is on stage alone, working out of a briefcase with a calculator and a list of share prices in the morning paper*

Mary enters L, *carrying a miniature malt whisky which she had hidden in the bracken. She stands over him*

Dylan studiously ignores her

Mary Oh, you're packing. (*Pause*) Beautifully. (*She waits for responses that don't come*) The others are down by the lake you know, and this is malt whisky. (*She peers out* R) I must say, Dylan, that really is a beautiful car you've got. (*Pause, sharply*) Someone's just dropped a brick wall on it! (*Pause*) How much was it? How much was it? How much was it? I shall keep going till you crack. How much was it?

Dylan First the carrot, now the tongue, eh?

Mary Now is there anything I can do to help. Apart from going to hell, that is.

Dylan suddenly rises in anger and Mary is frightened. She takes a step backwards

Dylan You can get off my back for a start! Please . . .

There is a slight pause

Mary (*smiling*) I've no intention of doing any such thing. (*Pause*) I had a tent once, as a girl. (*Beat*) And a rucksack. (*Beat*) I used to go off with a friend all the way down to the bottom of the garden. (*Beat*) If I were you I'd find that fascinating.

Dylan It's absolutely rivetting! The most rivetting thing the Western World has heard since . . .

Mary Ah! You were meant to argue so that I could counter with another totally irrelevant point.

There is a slight pause

Dylan You rehearse your conversations?

Mary The important ones. I was going to say "Have you managed to turn Apricot against me? After all I'd have thought you were *bully* enough. Just like me." (*Beat*) That little "just like me" was me being generous.

Dylan (*smiling*) And what did *I* say?

Mary You flung your arms round me and cried, "At last we have something in common." It was terribly moving.

Dylan Well . . . I'm sorry to have spoiled it. You'll have to fall back on saying the first thing that comes into your head.

Mary But that's been my trouble. It's never quite what I mean.

Dylan No, Mary . . . *your* trouble is that you're completely wrong about almost everything.

Mary (*beat*) Frank, of course, said I was terrified of you, didn't he?

Dylan Oh, Frank says, Frank says . . .

Mary What he didn't say is that *you're* terrified of *me*.

There is a slight pause

Dylan (*nodding*) Just a little.

Mary Now that *is* fascinating. That you and I, both cowards, meet like this, miles from home. When you think of how few cowards there must be in Wales at this very moment, why, we might have missed each other! (*Beat*) And that *would* have been a shame.

Dylan Really?

Mary Give me a cigarette and I'll tell you all about it. (*She smiles*) I've smoked all your others.

Dylan takes out a packet, looks at her and realizes that she is so drunk he'd better light it for her and does so

Mary I didn't ask you to smoke it for me as well. Swap you with a drink?

Dylan No. Thank you. (*He sticks the cigarette in her mouth and looks her in the eyes for a few moments. He speaks like Lauren Bacall*) You just put your lips together and pull.

Mary (*laughing*) Very good, Dylan. Aren't we getting on famously? Where was I?

Dylan We were all terrified but I didn't believe you.

Mary But you're scared out of your *wits*! Oh, for a very good reason, I know. Well I *think* I know.

Dylan You mean you think Frank thinks *he* knows.

Mary Not this time. What I'm struggling to say couldn't be said by a man. (*Beat*) Or even this woman, maybe. . . . It's a terrible strain for someone like me to think, you know. But one has to make an effort. And in the end I shouted "Biscuits" and the thought came running. "There's Dylan," I said to myself, "all on his tod. In the space of eight weeks he's leaped from being a boy who plays with runner beans and warehouses, right in the middle of a bear pit. Full of men. He's looked around and they have scared him *witless*. There they were, stooped at the shoulder, weighed down by all those cares . . . mortgages, wives, lawns which need mowing, children even . . ."

Dylan I'll cope.

Mary Well of course you will. We *all* will. But wouldn't it be nice to *enjoy* coping? Oh don't worry, if you don't like what I'm saying, blame it on Johnnie Walker. Everyone else does. (*Beat*) But you haven't drawn breath since she died.

There is a slight pause

Dylan No.

Mary There! That's the first straight answer you've given me since we started to fight. I mean I know we aren't fighting as such. But I'll bet you haven't even had a bloody good yell. Oh, I don't mean a chaste little sob and trickle when nobody's looking. I mean a full blown scream and shout at the world for taking her off. I mean it *is* their fault. They'll say it isn't, of course, but they're wrong.

Dylan I'm not the only person in the world whose mother died.

Mary True. Now you've taken her place. Overnight ... all in a snap. .... I won't snap the fingers ... I shall miss ... you became father, uncle, hunter and gatherer for your little sister. Why?

Dylan So that she ... (*He pauses ... tailing his voice off*)

Mary ... *needn't* be afraid? How lucky she is. I had a husband once who made me stoop. I took all the decisions, every damn one. From wallpaper to water rates. Shall we move there? Shall we do this? How about that? He wouldn't share and halve. He didn't see it as him and me against the world. Just me.

Dylan Poor world.

Mary What lovely teeth you have. (*Beat*) I'm a selfish cow, am I? Yes! So what's wrong with that? At least I don't enjoy being downtrodden. And those I take along for the ride don't get the chance to pull their faces either, because if Mary Challis calls you her friend, she insists that you straighten your back ... leave the stoop at the gate and become a friend for life. Do you know, if everyone was as selfish as me the world would be a better place. They'd look after things ... and the people they chose to be with. A vain, selfish, gang of four is a happier band than one kid from Acton, albeit with a Mercedes, going it alone for his baby sister. You, of course, agree entirely.

Dylan It makes sense, but no.

Mary really does *consider her next line carefully*

Mary I would never have put you down as old-fashioned, Dylan. But by God, you are. You're scared to break the mould and choose your own family.

Dylan To square your account with the world?

Mary (*smiling*) That's right. And to have such *fun* ... don't you see that?

Dylan I see talk.

Mary Well, me too, dear. The mad expression of an even madder idea. The least we should do is put it to the test. Move in with an old bat of a cabinet maker and a fuddy GP. Those stoopers out in the bear pit would run a mile at the idea. They think nothing in the world is reversible. They think so because they're gutless! And I tell you now that if we hate each other in a month's time, not only are you free to go, I'll kick you out myself.

Dylan We've missed the boat ... all of us. Let's just leave it at that.

Mary Rubbish! There *was* no boat! There *is now*! And ... (*beat*) ... Good heavens! With a stomach like mine these sea-faring analogies are quite disturbing.

Dylan (*quickly*) Bus! We missed the bus! Or didn't.

Mary The four of us have done things in the wrong order, just to be different, I expect. Frank and I spent our twenties and thirties growing old. I even came here to retire, remember? So ... with or without you my forties and fifties will be younger. You and Apricot spent your teens playing mother and father to Gillian Bartlett. Now it's your turn to be kids, maybe. But Dylan, those stoopers out in that bear pit, they do everything the "normal" way ... because they're dead up here. (*She taps* *her temple*) You and I ... *especially* you and I ... are not. And the last thing anyone could accuse me of being is "normal".

Dylan (*laughing*) Right!

Mary What a handsome boy you could be with a decent haircut. ... I'm sorry ... (*She smiles*) Slight regression there. (*She takes him by the shoulders*) I won't pretend to be your mother. Just call me Aunty ... though not in my hearing. (*Beat*) I've been halted in the process of running away, overjoyed at the prospect of having two people half my age to boast about at boring parties ... to lie about, to fight and scream at ... to fall in and out with.

Dylan puts his head on her shoulder

I'm a desperate old dragon. Tail's been docked and the fire's going out of my mouth. (*Beat*) Think about it. I promise it will be such fun. (*She goes to pull Dylan towards her*)

Dylan steps back and a moment later turns and exits hurriedly

Mary eventually sits in the chair Dylan has vacated, picks up his calculator, looks at it, presses a few buttons and holds it to her ear. She seems surprised that no music comes out

A moment or two passes, then Apricot enters L

Mary looks up at her and smiles. Apricot is far from cheerful

Apricot Hi!

Mary Hi! (*She rises*) Er ... what time is it?

Apricot (*teasing*) Twelv ... ish. As if you didn't know.

Mary As late as that. Must be nearly lunchtime. Right then, so where are we at ... as we used to say all those years ago.

Apricot Mary, what makes you think you're so out of date? Nobody invented a new language on your forty-second birthday. (*Beat*) The only old-fashioned person round here is Dylan.

Mary Well Frank is hardly Carnaby Street, is he?

Apricot (*puzzled*) Where? (*She helps herself to some food in the van*)

Mary You're starting on lunch?

Apricot Yes, I'm starving.

Mary Shouldn't we wait for the others?

Apricot Mary, it's not every day someone asks you to go and live with them.

Mary I should hope not! Just imagine hordes of childless people touring the country, tapping teenagers on the shoulders. "Excuse me, dear, I just wondered a) if you have a mother and b) are you satisfied with her because if not" ... I'm doing it again, aren't I?

Apricot Yeah!

Mary This could become quite a strain for me, you know. Halting myself in mid-spout.

Apricot You've made us such a good offer Mary, I'd like you to run it past me again.

Mary (*puzzled*) Where? Oh yes ... but suppose you say no?

Apricot I won't, I'll say yes. I'd just like to be asked again.

Mary Well ... how's this then? Do you fancy sharing my life? Equal partners, equal terms, equal shares. We'll catch up on all we missed. Could be such fun.

Apricot That's almost a straight question. It's a deal.

Mary (*anxiously*) Is that yes?

Apricot One down, one to go. (*She kisses Mary on the top of the head like a parent might do to a child*) So where's Boy Wonder?

Mary I hope he's gone off for a scream at the world. And not before time. Tell me, has Frank found another dilemma yet? I do hope so. He's never happy unless he can't make up his mind.

Apricot (*smiling*) He has. He swears he saw a buzzard on the other side of the lake.

Mary That was my alter-ego getting a breath of air.

Apricot I've told him it was a red kite but he won't have it.

Mary Who would fly a kite at this time of day? Mary Challis would. Mary Challis *did*.

Apricot Is Dylan coming with us?

Mary Dylan is deliberating.

Apricot Did you give him a deadline?

Mary I gave him a catalogue of all my weaknesses. I wonder if we'll ever see him again? I couldn't quite find the courage to say I could easily grow to ...

Apricot Love him?

Mary Oh good, the word is still in fashion.

Apricot So Mary is pretending to read. Don't worry, it happens to us all, but I promise you'll grow out of it.

Mary What?

Apricot This schoolgirl delirium to sit next to the boy of your dreams.

Mary I wonder if he knows about the glut of artichokes in Brazil? I must tell him.

Apricot Dylan will drive you mad, Mary. He'll take what's on offer, which in this case happens to be a family, and never mention it again. You weren't expecting him to thank you every day, were you?

Mary No, any more than I expected the offer to be tested so crudely. Here I am waiting on the nod or shake of a young man's head ... a man who's in no fit state to think, let alone do! I'm very bad at waiting. Dylan isn't. That is his strength. Stocks are running low. After this, it's back to the trees, I'm afraid.

Apricot Shall I get it down for you?

Mary Not yet, dear. One bottle on the go is sinful, two is rather flashy. What the hell is that boy playing at? I'll pretend to read again.

Apricot You'd make a rotten blackmailer, Mary.

Mary I know. Which way do you think he'll jump?

Dylan screams off

Apricot Over a cliff by the sound of it.

Frank enters in haste

Frank What was that?

Mary That was a common scream, Frank, as uttered by a young man about to change his life.

Frank I must go to him. He could ruin his sinuses if he does that again. Not many people know that.

Mary I wouldn't bother Frank. He's more likely to stampede the sheep than ruin his hooter. When we get him home, you can give him a thorough medical.

Frank Could you leave that alone for a while?

Mary No. This is the stuff that dreams are made of and right now it tells me that Dylan is ours. The more I have, the more I know it's true.

Apricot I'd better have some then!

Mary Frank, you'd better tell her what this does to the brain.

Frank I think she can see that for herself.

Apricot Give me!

Mary That must be short for please.

Apricot Yeah, with an "s" on the end.

Mary Frank, make a note in your diary. Dear Diary, today, the umpteenth of whatever . . .

Frank The twenty-second of August . . .

Mary . . . I, Frank Knight, took a wife and found a daughter, still waiting on a son. Frank, dear, you look worried. What do you think he'll say?

Frank He'll say no.

Mary Don't be absurd!

Frank Oh, very well, he'll say yes.

Mary That's better!

Apricot Frank, tell me, do you want us?

Mary Of course he does!

Apricot Oh, shut up, Mary, will you.

Mary Me?

Apricot We can all see that you want us but what about Frank?

Mary We, meaning I, meaning Frank, meaning we . . . speak as one.

Apricot Frank?

Frank Yes, I do.

Mary There, you see, what did I tell you? He's lost touch with a whole generation, you see. Young girls come to him every day with their problems and he tells them to come back in the morning. Why? So he can sneak home and ask my advice.

Frank True. And whatever she says, I counsel the opposite.

Mary Not true!

Frank It would be nice to have someone in the house who wasn't afraid of the future. Are you going to be doing A levels?

Apricot Physics, chemistry and maths.

Frank You should be a doctor!

Mary The last thing she wants to be is a doctor! I almost forbid it.

Frank I promise to sedate Mary as often as possible.

Apricot I thought about it.

Mary And rejected it!

Apricot Do go on, Frank!

Mary I will not tolerate sibling rivalry in my house.

Frank No, nor shall we.

Mary There will be no skulking in the corners or plotting with each other. We shall have an open forum on everything from breakfast to bank accounts. Oh, breakfast is at eight o'clock by the way.

Apricot What do we have? A lightly boiled scotch egg?

Mary Oh, very witty.

Apricot We don't eat breakfast.

Mary Well that's one thing that'll have to change. Where is that wretched boy? Frank, you said you'd go and see to him. You're becoming unreliable. I shall sit down. No I won't. I shall pack. When that boy walks into this room ... (*she looks up*) Oh God, now I'm seeing walls ... When he returns, that dreadful boy, maybe my dignity will return with him.

Apricot No matter what he says?

Dylan enters. He feels a lot better, in spite of the task before him

Dylan Right then.

Mary And where the bloody hell have *you* been? (*Beat*) You didn't pass my dignity on the road by any chance, did you?

Frank We heard a scream and ... well ... we wondered.

Dylan Wonder no more. You're wrong again Mary. The only thing screaming does is embarrass you.

Mary Dylan, before you start I have things to say, all wrapped up in proper sentences. It's just that I can't remember them. (*She smiles at him*) So, when do we leave?

Dylan Right now.

Mary (*delightedly*) I'll drive with you and Apricot. Frank can get this thing home on his own, can't you dear? (*Her brains have deserted her*) Can you? Can. Petrol can ... Frank, give the car a drink.

Frank, in his own time, fills the car from the can

Oh, Dylan, ever since you left to go for your scream, which I must compliment you on by the way ... simply blood curdling ... I have been like a bee in a bottle. I've been vile to Apricot, vile to my fiancé ... (*She laughs*) ... Frank a fiancé ... can you imagine it! And, of course, you don't have to eat breakfast if you don't want it. ... Who am I to tell two strapping adults what to do? I will tell you. I am your surrogate mother, slightly chipped and frayed around the edges, but I claim my prize. The only sound you'll ever hear from me is my make-up cracking when I smile. So ... in the spirit of true friendship, let us go east together ... and never stop till we reach that pearl in an otherwise unblemished oyster ... Aylesbury Civic Offices! From there we take the A418 to Thame, and turn off at the sign for Cuddington. Japanese volkswagons roll!

Dylan Mary ...

Mary Yes, dear ... ?

Dylan I know you're not as drunk as you make out. It's just a sandbag to hide behind in case whatever your mouth sets fire to burns the rest of us.

So think before you drink before you speak. (*Beat*) I'm not coming with you.

There is a pause

Mary (*by instinct*) Frank. Frank! (*Calmly*) Right. I'm thinking. How best to prevent the steam coming out of my ears.

Dylan (*turning to Apricot*) Come with me if you like. But you could knock the world off its feet, Ape. Go to some university or other. Don't drift around with me.

Frank Now just a minute, I thought ...

Dylan This is family, Frank. OK?

Frank I thought we nearly were.

Dylan According to the rule book, people of eighteen and twenty-one don't need parents.

Mary Seventeen and twenty.

Dylan The feeling is supposed to be mutual.

Frank The phrase "supposed to be" is driving the world insane, Dylan.

Dylan This is my family! (*He turns to Apricot*) Aylesbury's not on the edge of the world ... I can come and see you ... check out how you're doing ...

Apricot And you?

Dylan The house at Acton can go, if you don't want it.

Apricot nods

Don't know where I'll go then. A flat maybe. But I've got to have your blessing. You're all I've got.

Apricot (*quietly*) You can't wait to be shot of me. That's the truth isn't it?

Dylan (*to them all*) I'm sorry. Really I am.

Frank (*gently*) Dylan, no need. Just go. I'll help you. .... (*He packs whatever is left*)

Dylan (*to Mary*) Have I got your permission! Can I go free ... or are you going to tie me to the bumper?

Mary (*leaning off the van*) No. (*Kindly and sensibly*) This "thinking" business is very dangerous. It puts you in the absurd position of seeing someone else's point of view. There is a little voice inside, telling me what a fool you are. But you're not. It says I should get down on one knee and plead with you to join us. But the ground is wet. And my dignity has shrunk enough. So I won't. Maybe I should rattle on and sell the idea harder. But you're a businessman. You know a bad deal when you see one. So I won't. I could go further ... ask you what your mother would say. That would be unfair. I could promise to give up smoking, swearing, talking ... drinking. ...

Dylan No, don't.

Mary (*with a bottle in her hand*) I could empty this right here and now. But there's another in the trees. I could tell you to think of *me*. Me, me, me! That you're a selfish, frightened brat. But it isn't true. So I won't. I could bribe you with this ... or belt you over the head with it. (*She reaches into the van for the spoon*)

Dylan A spoon?

Mary A little ethnic gesture. On your way, bean baron. It was, as you say, only a dream, of which I still have half, I gather. And, in spite of the rule book, I'll settle for half. But ...! Should you change your mind ... well ...

Dylan The room over the conservatory, I think we said.

Mary I'll air the duvet. (*Beat*) Apricot, will you ever forgive me for splitting you up?

Apricot No need.

Mary Right! (*She lifts the mood*) How do you say goodbye to a son you only met on holiday ...?

Dylan shakes hands with Frank

Yes ... well I'd hardly expect you to hurl yourself into a clinch with *Frank*. But what about *me*?

Frank Good luck.

Mary Oh, is that what you say? Then good luck.

Dylan (*kissing Apricot on the cheek*) You've been drinking. Don't let it become ...

Mary She won't. Too smart.

Dylan So long, Dragon. (*He picks up his rucksack, with the tent tied to it. He heads for the exit, stops and turns to Mary*) I don't even know your address.

Mary The Red House. Cuddington. Near Aylesbury.

Dylan (*nodding*) The Red House.

Mary Matches my eyes, which you're avoiding.

Dylan Yeah!

Mary (*taking him by the shoulders*) I hereby ... what was it ...? Let you go free. Remember to shave, wash under your arms and be in bed by eleven! Keep in touch. Christmas at our house is wonderful ... could be such *fun.*

Dylan I'll bear it in mind ... (*He is about to put his head on her shoulder but decides against it*)

Dylan turns and exits hurriedly

Mary (*calling out after him*) Straighten your back!

Frank Why, what's wrong with it?

They stand and watch

The car door opens, closes, the engine fires and the car roars away

A moment or two later Mary galvanizes them into action with a single clap of her hands

Mary Right! Brace yourself Aylesbury! Mary's coming home!

Frank, to hide his disappointment, begins slinging their stuff in through the side door of the van

Home with Apricot and Frank ... are you all right, Frank?

Frank Just about.

Mary Apricot?

Apricot I should've moaned at him more when he was a kid. But instead I did something far worse.

Mary What was that?

Apricot I wouldn't let the poor little devil out of my sight. I ironed his underwear, embroidered his socks, did everything but chew his food for him. No wonder he's gone. It's the first time some female hasn't been two paces behind him.

Mary (*trying to brighten things*) Well . . . he'd have found me very different to that. Do I even *have* an iron, Frank?

Frank (*looking up from the packing, smiling*) Still two boards under the mattress, isn't it?

Mary As for chewing his food for him . . . do I *look* like a sparrow? Mind you, the socks bit I can understand. Feet have a very bad press. I'm all for brightening them up. You know, family, speaking on behalf of myself, since no one else seems willing to, I think I acquitted myself rather well then. I mean I know I lost . . . but didn't I do it nicely. . . . (*Beat*) Silly cow! I should have knocked his teeth out while I had them in reach! Oh, Frank. You've packed.

Frank I can always tip it out again if you're anxious to help.

Mary Now, shall I drive or will you? (*She smiles*) You can both raise your lower jaws because my vote goes to Frank. I've been drinking you see. Apricot, you sit in the front because I'm sure that in spite of everything I've said about this country it's probably rather beautiful. Like feet. And people.

Frank gets into the driver's seat and fires the engine. It is as dead as a doornail

Mary Frank, before I start spitting feathers, you do know that I'm in an emotional state, don't you? And that we always turn on the ones we love? So what is wrong with the van? Dear!

Frank Battery! If you could see your way clear to pushing me on to the road . . . I could coast and crash it into gear.

Mary (*quietly to Apricot*) So nice to see men and their machines in harmony. Apricot . . . you and I will move this van. Then we shall go on to move mountains.

Apricot (*cheering up*) Right!

Mary The brake *off* would help, Frank. . . .

Frank OK. Heave! Come on!

Mary and Apricot push the van from behind. Slowly it crawls off

Mary It'll be, "Great big girls like you should have no problem," any second now . . .

Frank (*off, shouting*) Girls like you! It should be a doddle!

Mary We'll beat him up when we get home.

Frank (*off, shouting*) We haven't left anything, have we?

Mary (*shouting back*) No dear. The round thing in front of you, Frank . . . needs a little twist to the left.

Frank (*off*) Right. Now this is all in the lap of the gods, you know.

Mary Don't get religious dear.
Frank (*off*) You sure we haven't left . . .
Mary Go!

Mary and Apricot exit

Apricot (*off*) What about the whisky?
Mary (*off*) To hell with it! (*Pause*) No, just a moment. Brake Frank!
(*Pause*) I mean it is fourteen pounds a bottle.
Frank (*off*) How much?
Mary (*off*) Well, it's old.
Frank (*off*) Well go and get it! Fourteen quid!

Mary enters, her attention still directed R *at Frank*

Mary Don't get shirty, Frank. Let's hope you're worth as much when
you're old and in a bottle. (*She pauses then looks around the clearing with
affection. She takes her time and finally has to smile and shrug off her own
absurdity. Eventually, she looks up to where the bottle should be . . . and is
puzzled by what she sees. She hurries to the tree, unties the knot, and slowly
lowers the string bag which now contains a small rock and a folded piece of
paper. The bag stops, she goes to it, removes the bag and takes out the
notepaper and reads it*) "Dear Dragon," (*That doesn't please her*) Hmm!
(*But she reads on*) "Only in the West are dragons feared. In the East
they're the Spirit of Change, of life itself; they live in pearl palaces and
speak in pleasant voices. Tie me to your bumper then it's yours sincerely,
The Expert; let me go free and I'll see you tonight in your palace. (*Beat*)
Which *could* make it . . . Love, Dylan." (*She folds the note carefully . . . she
begins to smile . . . she carries on till she has to verbalize . . . she clenches her
fist, punches it in the air and yells out something which can only be spelt
"Yee-harghhhh!"*)

CURTAIN

PRODUCTION NOTE

To overcome any difficulties in staging the van, with regard to its exit and entrance from the road, I suggest the following amendments. Even so, the van, however modest in size and mobility, will still need to be pushed off the collapsed tent.

D.W.

Act I, Scene 1

As the house lights go down we hear the sound of a storm which gives way to the approach of a car of some sort. It seems to be taking corners dangerously with much crashing of gears. It draws parallel with our hearing, stops, reverses and dies ...

The CURTAIN *rises ... to reveal the dead van with Mary and Frank sitting in it*

The engine is fired again and again but to no avail

Mary (*eventually*) Frank ... we seem to have stopped.
Frank I know! Petrol!
Mary Well there's no point in getting in a tizz. What did I say in Harlech? I said petrol. Any second now you'll blame me ...

Frank gets out of the car and slams the door hard. He peers out into the darkness

Where are you going? To drill for oil?
Frank What time is it?
Mary Quarter to twelve.

And then on as per script

The second alteration is needed in **Act II, Scene 2** (page 49)

Frank Battery! If you two could see your way clear to pushing me onto the road ... I could coast and crash it into gear.

Mary takes a bag from the van and swings it round on her shoulder

Mary Absolutely not, Frank! I have performed my last service for this wretched van of yours. There will be no pushing, coasting or crashing ...
Frank Do you have a better suggestion? It's a long way to Aylesbury.
Mary (*totally confident*) We shall hitch. Apricot, grab a few essentials in case we need to live off the land.

Apricot gets her rucksack from the van

Frank But you can't leave me here! In a foreign country!
Mary You're getting patriotic again, Frank. It doesn't suit ...

Mary takes Apricot by the hand and leads her off. Frank hastily locks the van and runs after them

Frank (*off*) Mary ... !
Apricot (*off*) You sure you haven't left anything?
Mary (*off*) Forward!
Apricot (*off*) What about the whisky?

And on as per script

FURNITURE AND PROPERTY LIST

ACT I

SCENE 1

On stage: Low, lightweight tent for two. *In it:* two rucksacks, assorted clothing and belongings including a skirt and a leather jacket, packet of cigarettes, bottle of vodka.

Off stage: Van. *In it:* Calor gas lamp, matches, map in a polythene bag, enormous flask of tea, holdall, bright orange picnic box containing sandwiches Pyjamas, old tartan dressing-gown, leather slippers, Doctor's bag, torch

Personal: **Frank:** yellow cycling cape, sou'wester
Mary: watch, sou'wester
Dylan: cigarettes and matches in pocket

SCENE 2

Set: Bottle of scotch in a string shopping bag, suspended from the tree
Two camping chairs by the van
Enormous pot of tea, plate of huge bacon sandwiches, mugs, plates, spoons, cutlery, sugar, sweetner dispenser
Petrol can in the back of the van

Off stage: Knife **(Frank)**
Large, black dustbin liner **(Dylan)**
Thin straight branch and a fat branch about eighteen inches long **(Mary)**

Personal: **Frank:** watch

ACT II

SCENE 1

Set: Wooden love spoon and carving knife for **Mary**
Make-up for **Apricot**

Off stage: Two packages, petrol can, newspaper **(Dylan)**

SCENE 2

Set: Briefcase, calculator and newspaper for **Dylan**
Small rock and a folded piece of paper in the string bag in place of the bottle of scotch

Personal: **Mary:** miniature malt whisky bottle
Dylan: cigarettes, matches in pocket

LIGHTING PLOT

Property fittings required: nil

Exterior. A clearing by a wooded lakeside. The same scene throughout

ACT I, SCENE 1.   Midnight

To open: Storm effect with occasional streaks of lightning, followed by a car's headlights approaching

Cue 1	As **Frank** measures the space available for his van *Sudden flash of lightning*	(Page 2)
Cue 2	As the back of the van reaches the tent *A flash or two of lightning*	(Page 2)
Cue 3	**Frank:** "The phone boxes." *Flash of lightning*	(Page 3)
Cue 4	**Mary** "... the moon up just a snatch?" *Lights up for a moonlight effect*	(Page 3)

ACT I, SCENE 2.   Early morning

To open: General lighting

No cues

ACT II, SCENE 1.   Morning

To open: General lighting

No cues

ACT II, SCENE 2.   Morning

To open: General lighting

No cues

EFFECTS PLOT

ACT I

Cue 1	At opening of Scene 1	(Page 1)
	A storm rages giving way to a van approaching dangerously, with much crashing of gears. The van arrives and the engine stalls and dies. After a few moments, the engine fires several times, but to no avail	
Cue 2	**Frank:** "I know! Petrol!"	(Page 1)
	Van door opens and slams shut	
Cue 3	Just after **Frank** exits	(Page 2)
	Van door opens and slams shut	
Cue 4	**Mary:** "Camden Town?"	(Page 2)
	Van door opens and slams shut	
Cue 5	**Frank:** "I'm sorry."	(Page 3)
	Clap of thunder	
Cue 6	**Frank:** "I'm a doctor!"	(Page 22)
	A car, far off, hoots once	
Cue 7	**Mary:** "Come with me!"	(Page 23)
	After a long pause, the sound of a car hooting a second time	
Cue 8	**Apricot:** "Gillian Bartlett was enough."	(Page 26)
	A car starts, far off, and moves nearer	
Cue 9	**Mary:** "He just can't manage it."	(Page 27)
	A car stops	
Cue 10	**Mary:** "But don't ever tell him I said so."	(Page 27)
	A car door opens and is slammed shut	
Cue 11	Just after **Dylan** exits	(Page 27)
	Car engine fires and then car drives away	

ACT II

Cue 12	**Apricot:** "Perrier water."	(Page 32)
	A car in the distance, approaching	
Cue 13	**Apricot:** "... to an even biddier little country."	(Page 32)
	Car stops	
Cue 14	As **Frank** and **Mary** stand and watch	(Page 48)
	Car door opens and closes followed by the engine firing and a car roaring away	

MADE AND PRINTED IN GREAT BRITAIN BY
LATIMER TREND & COMPANY LTD, PLYMOUTH
MADE IN ENGLAND